THE APPLE CART

A POLITICAL EXTRAVAGANZA

AF658607

GEORGE BERNARD SHAW

PEACOCK BOOKS

Published by
PEACOCK BOOKS
7/22, Ansari Road, Darya Ganj, New Delhi-110002
Phones : +91-11-40775252, 40775214, 23273880, 23275880
Fax : +91-11-23285873
Web : www.atlanticbooks.com
E-mail : orders@atlanticbooks.com

Peacock Books is an imprint of
Atlantic Publishers and Distributors (P) Ltd

First published 1929
Editorial and Design Copyright © Peacock Books, 2023

All rights reserved. No part of this publication may be reproduced, stored in a retrieval system, transmitted or utilized in any form or by any means, electronic, mechanical, photocopying, recording or otherwise, without the prior permission of the copyright owner. Application for such permission should be addressed to the publisher.
All disputes are subject to the jurisdiction of Delhi court only.

Printed & bound in India by Atlantic Print Services

PREFACE

The first performances of this play at home and abroad provoked several confident anticipations that it would be published with an elaborate prefatory treatise on Democracy to explain why I, formerly a notorious democrat, have apparently veered round to the opposite quarter and become a devoted Royalist. In Dresden the performance was actually prohibited as a blasphemy against Democracy.

What was all this pother about? I had written a comedy in which a King defeats an attempt by his popularly elected Prime Minister to deprive him of the right to influence public opinion through the press and the platform: in short, to reduce him to a cipher. The King's reply is that rather than be a cipher he will abandon his throne and take his obviously very rosy chance of becoming a popularly elected Prime Minister himself. To those who beli eve that our system of votes for everybody produces parliaments which represent the people it should seem that this solution of the difficulty is completely democratic, and that the Prime Minister must at once accept it joyfully as such. He knows better. The change would rally the anti-democratic royalist vote against him, and impose on him a rival in the person of the only public man whose ability he has to fear. The comedic paradox of the situation is that the King wins, not by exercising his royal authority, but by threatening to resign it and go to the democratic poll.

That so many critics who believe themselves to be ardent democrats should take the entirely personal triumph of the hereditary king over the elected minister to be a triumph of autocracy over democracy, and its dramatization an act of political apostasy on the part of the author, convinces me that our professed devotion to political principles is only a mask for our idolatry of eminent persons. The Apple Cart exposes the unreality of both democracy and royalty as our idealists conceive them. Our Liberal democrats believe in a figment called a constitutional monarch, a sort of Punch puppet who cannot move until his Prime Minister's fingers are in his sleeves. They believe in another figment called a responsible minister, who moves only when similarly actuated by the million fingers of the electorate. But the most superficial inspection of any two such figures shews that they are not puppets but living men, and that the supposed control of one by the other and of both by the electorate amounts to no more than a not very deterrent fear of uncertain and under ordinary circumstances quite remote consequences. The nearest thing to a puppet in our political system is a Cabinet minister at the head of a great public office. Unless he possesses a very exceptional share of dominating ability and relevant knowledge he is helpless in the hands of his officials. He must sign whatever documents they present to him, and repeat whatever words they put into his mouth when answering questions in parliament, with a docility which cannot be imposed on a King who works at his job; for the King works continuously whilst his ministers are in office for spells only, the spells being few and brief, and often occurring for the first time to men of advanced age with little or no training for and experience of supreme responsibility. George the Third and Queen Victoria were not, like Queen Elizabeth, the natural superiors of their ministers in political genius and general capacity; but they were for many purposes of State necessarily superior to them in experience, in cunning, in exact knowledge of the limits of their responsibility and consequently of the limits of their irresponsibility: in short, in the authority and practical power that these superiorities produce. Very clever men who have come into contact with monarchs have been so impressed that they have attributed to them extraordinary natural qualifications which they, as now visible to us in historical perspective, clearly did not possess. In conflicts between monarchs and popularly elected ministers the monarchs win every time when personal ability and good sense are at all equally divided.

In The Apple Cart this equality is assumed. It is masked by a strong contrast of character and methods which has led my less considerate critics to complain that I have packed the cards by making the King a wise man and the minister a fool. But that is not at all the relation between the two. Both play with equal skill; and the King wins, not by greater astuteness, but because he has the ace of trumps in his hand and knows when to play it. As the prettier player of the two he has the sympathy of the audience. Not being as pampered and powerful as an operatic prima donna, and depending as he does not on some commercially valuable talent but on his conformity to the popular ideal of dignity and perfect breeding, he has to be trained, and to train himself, to accept good manners as an indispensable condition of his intercourse with his subjects, and to leave to the less highly placed such indulgences as tempers, tantrums, bullyings, sneerings, swearings, kickings: in short, the commoner violences and intemperances of authority.

His ministers have much laxer standards. It is open to them, if it will save their time, to get their own way by making scenes, flying into calculated rages, and substituting vulgar abuse for argument. A clever minister, not having had a royal training, will, if he finds himself involved in a duel with his King, be careful not to choose the weapons at which the King can beat him. Rather will he in cold blood oppose to the king's perfect behavior an intentional misbehavior and apparently childish petulance which he can always drop at the right moment for a demeanor as urbane as that of the king himself, thus, employing two sets of weapons to the king's one. This gives him the advantages of his own training as a successful ambitious man who has pushed his way from obscurity to celebrity: a process involving a considerable use of the shorter and more selfish methods of dominating the feebly recalcitrant, the unreasonable, the timid, and the stupid, as well as a sharp sense of the danger of these methods when dealing with persons of strong character in strong positions.

In this light the style of fighting adopted by the antagonists in the scrap between King Magnus and Mr. Joseph Proteus is seen to be a plain deduction from their relative positions and antecedents, and not a manufactured contrast between democracy and royalty to the disadvantage of the former. Those who so mistook it are out of date. They still regard democracy as the under dog in the conflict. But to me it is the king who is doomed to be tragically in that position in the future into which the play is projected: in fact, he is visibly at least half in it already; and the theory of constitutional monarchy assumes that he is wholly in it, and has been so since the end of the seventeenth century.

Besides, the conflict is not really between royalty and democracy. It is between both and plutocracy, which, having destroyed the royal power by frank force under democratic pretexts, has bought and swallowed democracy. Money talks: money prints: money broadcasts: money reigns; and kings and labor leaders alike have to register its decrees, and even, by a staggering paradox, to finance its enterprises and guarantee its profits. Democracy is no longer bought: it is bilked. Ministers who are Socialists to the backbone are as helpless in the grip of Breakages Limited as its acknowledged henchmen: from the moment when they attain to what is with unintentional irony called power (meaning the drudgery of carrying on for the plutocrats) they no longer dare even to talk of nationalizing any industry, however socially vital, that has a farthing of profit for plutocracy still left in it, or that can be made to yield a farthing for it by subsidies.

King Magnus's little tactical victory, which bulks so largely in the playhouse, leaves him in a worse plight than his defeated opponent, who can always plead that he is only the instrument of the people's will, whereas the unfortunate monarch, making a desperate bid for dictatorship on the perfectly true plea that democracy has destroyed all other responsibility (has not Mussolini said that there is a vacant throne in every country in Europe waiting for a capable man to fill it?), is compelled to assume full responsibility himself, and face all the reproaches that Mr. Proteus can shirk. In his Cabinet there is only one friendly man who has courage, principle, and genuine good manners when he is courteously treated; and that man is an uncompromising republican, his rival for the dictatorship. The splendidly honest and devoted Die-hard lady is too scornfully tactless to help much;

but with a little more experience in the art of handling effective men and women as distinguished from the art of handling mass meetings Mr. Bill Boanerges might surprise those who, because he makes them laugh, see nothing in him but a caricature.

In short, those critics of mine who have taken The Apple Cart for a story of a struggle between a hero and a roomful of guys have been grossly taken in. It is never safe to take my plays at their suburban face value: it ends in your finding in them only what you bring to them, and so getting nothing for your money.

On the subject of Democracy generally I have nothing to say that can take the problem farther than I have already carried it in my Intelligent Woman's Guide to Socialism and Capitalism. We have to solve two inseparable main problems: the economic problem of how to produce and distribute our subsistence, and the political problem of how to select our rulers and prevent them from abusing their authority in their own interests or those of their class or religion. Our solution of the economic problem is the Capitalist system, which achieves miracles in production, but fails so ludicrously and disastrously to distribute its products rationally, or to produce in the order of social need, that it is always complaining of being paralysed by its "overproduction" of things of which millions of us stand in desperate want. Our solution of the political problem is Votes for Everybody and Every Authority Elected by Vote, an expedient originally devised to prevent rulers from tyrannizing by the very effectual method of preventing them from doing anything, and thus leaving everything to irresponsible private enterprise. But as private enterprise will do nothing that is not profitable to its little self, and the very existence of civilization now depends on the swift and unhampered public execution of enterprises that supersede private enterprise and are not merely profitable but vitally necessary to the whole community, this purely inhibitive check on tyranny has become a stranglehold on genuine democracy. Its painfully evolved machinery of parliament and Party System and Cabinet is so effective in obstruction that we take thirty years by constitutional methods to do thirty minutes work, and shall presently be forced to clear up thirty years arrears in thirty minutes by unconstitutional ones unless we pass a Reform Bill that will make a complete revolution in our political machinery and procedure. When we see parliaments like ours kicked into the gutter by dictators, both in kingdoms and republics, it is foolish to wait until the dictator dies or collapses, and then do nothing but pick the poor old things up and try to scrape the mud off them: the only sane course is to take the step by which the dictatorship could have been anticipated and averted, and construct a political system for rapid positive work instead of slow nugatory work, made to fit into the twentieth century instead of into the sixteenth.

Until we face this task and accomplish it we shall not be able to produce electorates capable of doing anything by their votes except pave the way to their own destruction. An election at present, considered as a means of selecting the best qualified rulers, is so absurd that if the last dozen parliaments had consisted of the candidates who were at the foot of the poll instead of those who were at the head of it there is no reason to suppose that we should have been a step more or less advanced than we are today. In neither case would the electorate have had any real choice of representatives. If it had, we might have had to struggle with parliaments of Titus Oateses and Lord George Gordons dominating a few generals and artists, with Cabinets made up of the sort of orator who is said to carry away his hearers by his eloquence because, having first ascertained by a few cautious feelers what they are ready to applaud, he gives it to them a dozen times over in an overwhelming crescendo, and is in effect carried away by them. As it is, the voters have no real choice of candidates: they have to take what they can get and make the best of it according to their lights, which is often the worst of it by the light of heaven. By chance rather than by judgment they find themselves represented in parliament by a fortunate proportion of reasonably honest and public spirited persons who happen to be also successful public speakers. The rest are in parliament because they can afford it and have a fancy for it or an interest in it.

Last October (1929) I was asked to address the enormous audience created by the new invention of Wireless Broadcast on a range of political and cultural topics introduced by a previous speaker under the general heading of Points of View. Among the topics was Democracy, presented, as usual, in a completely abstract guise as an infinitely beneficent principle in which we must trust though it slay us. I was determined that this time Votes for Everybody and Every Authority Elected by Vote should not escape by wearing its imposing mask. I delivered myself as follows:

Your Majesties, your Royal Highnesses, your Excellencies, your Graces and Reverences, my Lords, Ladies and Gentlemen, fellow-citizens of all degrees: I am going to talk to you about Democracy objectively: that is, as it exists and as we must all reckon with it equally, no matter what our points of view may be. Suppose I were to talk to you not about Democracy, but about the sea, which is in some respects rather like Democracy! We all have our own views of the sea. Some of us hate it and are never well when we are at it or on it. Others love it, and are never so happy as when they are in it or on it or looking at it. Some of us regard it as Britain's natural realm and surest bulwark: others want a Channel Tunnel. But certain facts about the sea are quite independent of our feelings towards it. If I take it for granted that the sea exists, none of you will contradict me. If I say that the sea is sometimes furiously violent and always uncertain, and that those who are most familiar with it trust it least, you will not immediately shriek out that I do not believe in the sea; that I am an enemy of the sea; that I want to abolish the sea; that I am going to make bathing illegal; that I am out to ruin our carrying trade and lay waste all our seaside resorts and scrap the British Navy. If I tell you that you cannot breathe in the sea, you will not take that as a personal insult and ask me indignantly if I consider you inferior to a fish. Well, you must please be equally sensible when I tell you some hard facts about Democracy. When I tell you that it is sometimes furiously violent and always dangerous and treacherous, and that those who are familiar with it as practical statesmen trust it least, you must not at once denounce me as a paid agent of Benito Mussolini, or declare that I have become a Tory Die-hard in my old age, and accuse me of wanting to take away your votes and make an end of parliament, and the franchise, and free speech, and public meeting, and trial by jury. Still less must you rise in your places and give me three rousing cheers as a champion of medieval monarchy and feudalism. I am quite innocent of any such extravagances. All I mean is that whether we are Democrats or Tories, Catholics or Protestants, Communists or Fascists, we are all face to face with a certain force in the world called Democracy; and we must understand the nature of that force whether we want to fight it or to forward it. Our business is not to deny the perils of Democracy, but to provide against them as far as we can, and then consider whether the risks we cannot provide against are worth taking.

Democracy, as you know it, is seldom more than a long word beginning with a capital letter, which we accept reverently or disparage contemptuously without asking any questions. Now we should never accept anything reverently until we have asked it a great many very searching questions, the first two being What are you? and Where do you live? When I put these questions to Democracy the answer I get is "My name is Demos; and I live in the British Empire, the United States of America, and wherever the love of liberty burns in the heart of man. You, my friend Shaw, are a unit of Democracy: your name is also Demos: you are a citizen of a great democratic community: you are a potential constituent of the Parliament of Man, The Federation of the World." At this I usually burst into loud cheers, which do credit to my enthusiastic nature. To-night, however, I shall do nothing of the sort: I shall say "Dont talk nonsense. My name is not Demos: it is Bernard Shaw. My address is not the British Empire, nor the United States of America, nor wherever the love of liberty burns in the heart of man: it is at such and such a number in such and such a street in London; and it will be time enough to discuss my seat in the Parliament of Man when that celebrated institution comes into existence. I dont believe your name is Demos: nobody's name is Demos; and all I can make of your address is that you have no address and are just a tramp—if indeed you exist at all."

You will notice that I am too polite to call Demos a windbag or a hot air merchant; but I am going to ask you to begin our study of Democracy by considering it first as a big balloon, filled with gas or hot air, and sent up so that you shall be kept looking up at the sky whilst other people are picking your pockets. When the balloon comes down to earth every five years or so you are invited to get into the basket if you can throw out one of the people who are sitting tightly in it; but as you can afford neither the time nor the money, and there are forty millions of you and hardly room for six hundred in the basket, the balloon goes up again with much the same lot in it and leaves you where you were before. I think you will admit that the balloon as an image of Democracy corresponds to the parliamentary facts.

Now let us examine a more poetic conception of Democracy. Abraham Lincoln is represented as standing amid the carnage of the battlefield of Gettysburg, and declaring that all that slaughter of Americans by Americans occurred in order that Democracy, defined as government *of* the people *for* the people *by* the people, should not perish from the earth. Let us pick this famous peroration to pieces and see what there really is inside it. (By the way, Lincoln did not really declaim it on the field of Gettysburg; and the American Civil War was not fought in defence of any such principle, but, on the contrary, to enable one half of the United States to force the other half to be governed as they did not wish to be governed. But never mind that. I mentioned it only to remind you that it seems impossible for statesmen to make speeches about Democracy, or journalists to report them, without obscuring it in a cloud of humbug.)

Now for the three articles of the definition. Number One: Government of the people: that, evidently, is necessary: a human community can no more exist without a government than a human being can exist without a co-ordinated control of its breathing and blood circulation. Number Two: Government *for* the people, is most important. Dean Inge put it perfectly for us when he called Democracy a form of society which means equal consideration for all. He added that it is a Christian principle, and that, as a Christian, he believes in it. So do I. That is why I insist on equality of income. Equal consideration for a person with a hundred a year and one with a hundred thousand is impossible. Number Three: Government *by* the people, is quite a different matter. All the monarchs, all the tyrants, all the dictators, all the Die-hard Tories are agreed that we must be governed. Democrats like the Dean and myself are agreed that we must be governed with equal consideration for everybody. But we repudiate Number Three on the ground that the people cannot govern. The thing is a physical impossibility. Every citizen cannot be a ruler any more than every boy can be an engine driver or a pirate king. A nation of prime ministers or dictators is as absurd as an army of field marshals. Government by the people is not and never can be a reality: it is only a cry by which demagogues humbug us into voting for them. If you doubt this—if you ask me "Why should not the people make their own laws?" I need only ask you "Why should not the people write their own plays?" They cannot. It is much easier to write a good play than to make a good law. And there are not a hundred men in the world who can write a play good enough to stand daily wear and tear as long as a law must.

Now comes the question, If we cannot govern ourselves, what can we do to save ourselves from being at the mercy of those who *can* govern, and who may quite possibly be thoroughpaced grafters and scoundrels? The primitive answer is that as we are always in a huge majority we can, if rulers oppress us intolerably, burn their houses and tear them to pieces. This is not satisfactory.

Decent people never do it until they have quite lost their heads; and when they have lost their heads they are as likely as not to burn the wrong house and tear the wrong man to pieces. When we have what is called a popular movement very few people who take part in it know what it is all about. I once saw a real popular movement in London. People were running excitedly through the streets. Everyone who saw them doing it immediately joined in the rush. They ran simply because everyone else was doing it. It was most impressive to see thousands of people sweeping along at full speed like that. There could be no doubt that it was literally a popular movement. I ascertained afterwards that it was started by a runaway cow. That cow had an important share in my education as a political philosopher; and I can assure you that if you will study crowds, and lost and terrified animals, and things like that, instead of reading books and newspaper articles, you will learn a great deal about politics from them. Most general elections, for instance, are nothing but stampedes. Our last but one was a conspicuous example of this. The cow was a Russian one.

I think we may take it that neither mob violence nor popular movements can be depended on as checks upon the abuse of power by governments. One might suppose that at least they would act as a last resort when an autocrat goes mad and commits outrageous excesses of tyranny and cruelty. But it is a curious fact that they never do. Take two famous cases: those of Nero and Tsar Paul the First of Russia. If Nero had been an ordinary professional fiddler he would probably have been no worse a man than any member of the wireless orchestra. If Paul had been a lieutenant in a line regiment we should never have heard of him. But when these two poor fellows were invested with absolute powers over their fellow-creatures they went mad, and did such appalling things that they had to be killed like mad dogs. Only, it was not the people that rose up and killed them. They were dispatched quite privately by a very select circle of their own bodyguards. For a genuinely democratic execution of unpopular statesmen we must turn to the brothers De Witt, who were torn to pieces by a Dutch mob in the seventeenth century. They were neither tyrants nor autocrats. On the contrary, one of them had been imprisoned and tortured for his resistance to the despotism of William of Orange; and the other had come to meet him as he came out of prison. The mob was on the side of the autocrat. We may take it that the shortest way for a tyrant to get rid of a troublesome champion of liberty is to raise a hue and cry against him as an unpatriotic person and leave the mob to do the rest after supplying them with a well tipped ringleader. Nowadays this is called direct action by the revolutionary proletariat. Those who put their faith in it soon find that proletariats are never revolutionary, and that their direct action, when it is controlled at all, is usually controlled by police agents.

Democracy, then, cannot be government by the people: it can only be government by consent of the governed. Unfortunately, when democratic statesmen propose to govern us by our own consent, they find that we dont want to be governed at all, and that we regard rates and taxes and rents and death duties as intolerable burdens. What we want to know is how little government we can get along with without being murdered in our beds. That question cannot be answered until we have explained what we mean by getting along. Savages manage to get along. Unruly Arabs and Tartars get along. The only rule in the matter is that the civilized way of getting along is the way of corporate action, not individual action; and corporate action involves more government than individual action.

Thus, government, which used to be a comparatively simple affair, today has to manage an enormous development of Socialism and Communism. Our industrial and social life is set in a huge communistic framework of public roadways, streets, bridges, water supplies, power supplies, lighting, tramways, schools, dockyards, and public aids and conveniences, employing a prodigious army of police, inspectors, teachers, and officials of all grades in hundreds of departments. We have found by bitter experience that it is impossible to trust factories, workshops, and mines to private management. Only by stern laws enforced by constant inspection have we stopped the monstrous waste of human life and welfare it cost when it was left uncontrolled by the Government. During the war our attempt to leave the munitioning of the army to private enterprise led us to the verge of defeat and caused an appalling slaughter of our soldiers. When the Government took the work out of private hands and had it done in national factories it was at once successful. The private firms were still allowed to do what little they could; but they had to be taught to do it economically, and to keep their accounts properly, by Government officials. Our big capitalist enterprises now run to the Government for help as a lamb runs to its mother. They cannot even make an extension of the Tube railway in London without Government aid. Unassisted private capitalism is breaking down or getting left behind in all directions. If all our Socialism and Communism and the drastic taxation of unearned incomes which finances it were to stop, our private enterprises would drop like shot stags, and we should all be dead in a month. When Mr. Baldwin tried to win the last election by declaring that Socialism had been a failure whenever and wherever it had been tried, Socialism went over him like a steam roller and handed his office to a Socialist Prime Minister. Nothing could save us in the war but a great extension of Socialism; and now it is clear enough that only still greater extensions of it can repair the ravages of the war and keep pace with the growing requirements of civilization.

What we have to ask ourselves, then, is not whether we will have Socialism and Communism or not, but whether Democracy can keep pace with the developments of both that are being forced on us by the growth of national and international corporate action.

Now corporate action is impossible without a governing body. It may be the central Government: it may be a municipal corporation, a county council, a district council, or a parish council. It may be the board of directors of a joint stock company, or of a trust made by combining several joint stock companies. Such boards, elected by the votes of the shareholders, are little States within the State, and very powerful ones, too, some of them. If they have not laws and kings, they have by-laws and chairmen. And you and I, the consumers of their services, are more at the mercy of the boards that organize them than we are at the mercy of parliament. Several active politicians who began as Liberals and are now Socialists have said to me that they were converted by seeing that the nation had to choose, not between governmental control of industry and control by separate private individuals kept in order by their competition for our custom, but between governmental control and control by gigantic trusts wielding great power without responsibility, and having no object but to make as much money out of us as possible. Our Government is at this moment having much more trouble with the private corporations on whom we are dependent for our coals and cotton goods than with France or the United States of America. We are in the hands of our corporate bodies, public or private, for the satisfaction of our everyday needs. Their powers are life and death powers. I need not labor this point: we all know it.

But what we do not all realize is that we are equally dependent on corporate action for the satisfaction of our religious needs. Dean Inge tells us that our general elections have become public auctions at which the contending parties bid against one another for our votes by each promising us a larger share than the other of the plunder of the minority. Now that is perfectly true. The contending parties do not as yet venture to put it exactly in those words; but that is what it comes to. And the Dean's profession obliges him to urge his congregation, which is much wider than that of St. Paul's (it extends across the Atlantic), always to vote for the party which pledges itself to go farthest in enabling those of us who have great possessions to sell them and give the price to the poor. But we cannot do this as private persons. It must be done by the Government or not at all. Take my own case. I am not a young man with great possessions; but I am an old man paying enough income tax and surtax to provide doles for some hundreds of unemployed and old age pensioners. I have not the smallest objection to this: on the contrary, I advocated it strongly for years before I had any income worth taxing. But I could not do it if the Government did not arrange it for me. If the Government ceased taxing my superfluous money and redistributing it among people who have no incomes at all, I could do nothing by myself. What could I do? Can you suggest anything? I could send my war bonds to the Chancellor of the Exchequer and invite him to cancel the part of the National Debt that they represent; and he would undoubtedly thank me in the most courteous official terms for my patriotism. But the poor would not get any of it. The other payers of surtax and income tax and death duties would save the interest they now have to pay on it: that is all. I should only have made the rich richer and myself poorer. I could burn all my share certificates and inform the secretaries of the companies that they might write off that much of their capital indebtedness. The result would be a bigger dividend for the rest of the shareholders, with the poor out in the cold as before. I might sell my war bonds and share certificates for cash and throw the money into the street to be scrambled for; but it would be snatched up, not by the poorest, but by the best fed and most able-bodied of the scramblers. Besides, if we all tried to sell our bonds and shares—and this is what you have to consider; for Christ's advice was not addressed to me alone but to all who have great possessions—the result would be that their value would fall to nothing, as the Stock Exchange would immediately become a market in which there were all sellers and no buyers. Accordingly, any spare money that the Government leaves me is invested where I can get the highest interest and the best security, as thereby I can make sure that it goes where it is most wanted and gives immediate employment. This is the best I can do without Government interference: indeed any other way of dealing with my spare money would be foolish and demoralizing; but the result is that I become richer and richer, and the poor become relatively poorer and poorer. So you see I cannot even be a Christian except through Government action; and neither can the Dean.

Now let us get down to our problem. We cannot govern ourselves; yet if we entrust the immense powers and revenues which are necessary in an effective modern

Government to an absolute monarch or dictator, he goes more or less mad unless he is a quite extraordinary and therefore very seldom obtainable person. Besides, modern government is not a one-man job: it is too big for that. If we resort to a committee or parliament of superior persons, they will set up an oligarchy and abuse their power for their own benefit. Our dilemma is that men in the lump cannot govern themselves; and yet, as William Morris put it, no man is good enough to be another man's master. We need to be governed, and yet to control our governors. But the best governors will not accept any control except that of their own consciences; and, as we who are governed are also apt to abuse any power of control we have, our ignorance, our passions, our private and immediate interests are constantly in conflict with the knowledge, the wisdom, and the public spirit and regard for the future of our best qualified governors.

Still, if we cannot control our governors, can we not at least choose them and change them if they do not suit?

Let me invent a primitive example of democratic choice. It is always best to take imaginary examples: they offend nobody. Imagine then that we are the inhabitants of a village. We have to elect somebody for the office of postman. There are several candidates; but one stands out conspicuously, because he has frequently treated us at the public-house, has subscribed a shilling to our little flower show, has a kind word for the children when he passes, and is a victim of oppression by the squire because his late father was one of our most successful poachers. We elect him triumphantly; and he is duly installed, uniformed, provided with a red bicycle, and given a batch of letters to deliver. As his motive in seeking the post has been pure ambition, he has not thought much beforehand about his duties; and it now occurs to him for the first time that he cannot read. So he hires a boy to come round with him and read the addresses. The boy conceals himself in the lane whilst the postman delivers the letters at the house, takes the Christmas boxes, and gets the whole credit of the transaction. In course of time he dies with a high reputation for efficiency in the discharge of his duties; and we elect another equally illiterate successor on similar grounds. But by this time the boy has grown up and become an institution. He presents himself to the new postman as an established and indispensable feature of the postal system, and finally becomes recognized and paid by the village as such.

Here you have the perfect image of a popularly elected Cabinet Minister and the Civil Service department over which he presides. It may work very well; for our postman, though illiterate, may be a very capable fellow; and the boy who reads the addresses for him may be quite incapable of doing anything more. But this does not always happen. Whether it happens or not, the system is not a democratic reality: it is a democratic illusion. The boy, when he has ability to take advantage of the situation, is the master of the man. The person elected to do the work is not really doing it: he is a popular humbug who is merely doing what a permanent official tells him to do. That is how it comes about that we are now governed by a Civil Service which has such enormous power that its regulations are taking the place of the laws of England, though some of them are made for the convenience of the officials without the slightest regard to the convenience or even the rights of the public. And how are our Civil Servants selected? Mostly by an educational test which nobody but an expensively schooled youth can pass, thus making the most powerful and effective part of our government an irresponsible class government.

Now, what control have you or I over the Services? We have votes. I have used mine a few times to see what it is like. Well, it is like this. When the election approaches, two or three persons of whom I know nothing write to me soliciting my vote and enclosing a list of meetings, an election address, and a polling card. One of the addresses reads like an article in *The Morning Post*, and has a Union Jack on it. Another is like *The Daily News* or *Manchester Guardian*. Both might have been compiled from the editorial waste paper baskets of a hundred years ago. A third address, more up-to-date and much better phrased, convinces me that the sender has had it written for him at the headquarters of the Labor Party. A fourth, the most hopelessly out of date of them all, contains scraps of the early English translations of the Communist Manifesto of 1848. I have no guarantee that any of these documents were written by the candidates. They convey nothing whatever to me as to their character or political capacity. The half-tone photographic portraits which adorn the front pages do not even tell me their ages, having been taken twenty years ago. If I go to one of the meetings I find a schoolroom packed with people who find an election meeting cheaper and funnier than a theatre. On the platform sit one or two poor men who have worked hard to keep party politics alive in the constituency. They ought to be the candidates; but they have no more chance of such eminence than they have of possessing a Rolls-Royce car. They move votes of confidence in the candidate, though as the candidate is a stranger to them and to everybody else present nobody can possibly feel any such confidence. They lead the applause for him; they prompt him when questions are asked; and when he is completely floored they jump up and cry "Let me answer that, Mr. Chairman!" and then pretend that he has answered it. The old shibboleths are droned over; and nothing has any sense or reality in it except the vituperation of the opposition party, which is received with shouts of relief by the audience. Yet it is nothing but an exhibition of bad manners. If I vote for one of these candidates, and he or she is elected, I am supposed to be enjoying a democratic control of the government—to be exercising government *of* myself, *for* myself, *by* myself. Do you wonder that the Dean cannot believe such nonsense? If I believed it I should not be fit to vote at all. If this is Democracy, who can blame Signor Mussolini for describing it as a putrefying corpse?

The candidates may ask me what more they can do for me but present themselves and answer any questions I may put to them. I quite admit that they can do nothing; but that does not mend matters. What I should like is a real test of their capacity. Shortly before the war a doctor in San Francisco discovered that if a drop of a candidate's blood can be obtained on a piece of blotting paper it is possible to discover within half an hour what is wrong with him physically. What I am waiting for is the discovery of a process by which on delivery of a drop of his blood or a lock of his hair we can ascertain what is right with him mentally. We could then have a graded series of panels of capable persons for all employments, public or private, and not allow any person, however popular, to undertake the employment of governing us unless he or she were on the appropriate panel. At the lower end of the scale there would be a panel of persons qualified to take part in a parish meeting; at the higher end a panel of persons qualified to act as Secretaries of State for Foreign Affairs or Finance Ministers. At present not more than two per thousand of the population would be available for the highest panel. I should then be in no danger of electing a postman and finding that he could neither read nor write. My choice of candidates would be perhaps more restricted than at present; but I do not desire liberty to choose windbags and nincompoops to represent me in parliament; and my power to choose between one qualified candidate and another would give me as much control as is either possible or desirable. The voting and counting would be done by machinery: I should connect my telephone with the proper office; touch a button; and the machinery would do the rest.

Pending such a completion of the American doctor's discovery, how are we to go on? Well, as best we can, with the sort of government that our present system produces. Several reforms are possible without any new discovery. Our present parliament is obsolete: it can no more do the work of a modern State than Julius Caesar's galley could do the work of an Atlantic liner. We need in these islands two or three additional federal legislatures, working on our municipal committee system instead of our parliamentary party system. We need a central authority to co-ordinate the federal work. Our obsolete little internal frontiers must be obliterated, and our units of local government enlarged to dimensions compatible with the recent prodigious advances in facility of communication and co-operation. Commonwealth affairs and super-national activities through the League of Nations or otherwise will have to be provided for, and Cabinet function to be transformed. All the pseudo-democratic obstructive functions of our political machinery must be ruthlessly scrapped, and the general problem of government approached from a positive viewpoint at which mere anarchic national sovereignty as distinguished from self-government will have no meaning.

I must conclude by warning you that when everything has been done that can be done, civilization will still be dependent on the consciences of the governors and the governed. Our natural dispositions may be good; but we have been badly brought up and are full of anti-social personal ambitions and prejudices and snobberies. Had we not better teach our children to be better citizens than ourselves? We are not doing that at present. The Russians *are*. That is my last word. Think over it.

So much for my broadcast on Democracy! And now a word about Breakages, Limited. Like all Socialists who know their business I have an exasperated sense of the mischief done by our system of private Capitalism in setting up huge vested interests in destruction, waste, and disease. The armament firms thrive on war; the glaziers gain by broken windows; the operating surgeons depend on cancer for their children's bread; the distillers and brewers build cathedrals to sanctify the profits of drunkenness; and the prosperity of Dives costs the privation of a hundred Lazaruses.

The title Breakages, Limited, was suggested to me by the fate of that remarkable genius, the late Alfred Warwick Gattie, with whom I was personally acquainted. I knew him first as the author of a play. He was a disturbing man, afflicted—or, as it turned out, gifted—with chronic hyperæsthesia, feeling everything violently and expressing his feelings vehemently and on occasion volcanically. I concluded that he was not sufficiently cold-blooded to do much as a playwright; so that when, having lost sight of him for some years, I was told that he had made an invention of first-rate importance, I was incredulous, and concluded that the invention was only a Utopian project. Our friend Henry Murray was so provoked by my attitude that to appease him I consented to investigate the alleged great invention in person on Gattie's promising to behave like a reasonable being during the process, a promise which he redeemed with the greatest dignity, remaining silent whilst an engineer explained his miracles to me, and contenting himself with the reading of a brief statement shewing that the adoption of his plan would release from industry enough men to utterly overwhelm the Central Empires with whom we were then at war.

I approached the investigation very sceptically. Our friend spoke of "the works." I could not believe that Gattie had any works, except in his fervid imagination. He mentioned "the company." That was more credible: anyone may form a company; but that it had any resources seemed to me doubtful. However, I suffered myself to be taken to Battersea; and there, sure enough, I found a workshop, duly labelled as the premises of The New Transport Company, Limited, and spacious enough to accommodate a double railway line with a platform. The affair was unquestionably real, so far. The platform was not provided with a station: its sole equipment was a table with a row of buttons on it for making electrical contacts. Each line of railway had on it a truck with a steel lid. The practical part of the proceedings began by placing an armchair on the lid of one of the trucks and seating me in it. A brimming glass of water was then set at my feet. I could not imagine what I was expected to do with the water or what was going to happen; and there was a suggestion of electrocution about the chair which made me nervous. Gattie then sat down majestically at the table on the platform with his hand hovering over the buttons. Intimating that the miracle would take place when my truck passed the other truck, he asked me to choose whether it should occur at the first passage or later, and to dictate the order in which it should be repeated. I was by that time incapable of choosing; so I said the sooner the better; and the two trucks started. When the other truck had passed mine I found myself magically sitting on it, chair and all, with the glass of water unspilled at my feet.

The rest of the story is a tragi-comedy. When I said to Gattie apologetically (I felt deeply guilty of having underrated him) that I had never known that he was an engineer, and had taken him to be the usual amateur inventor with no professional training, he told me that this was exactly what he was: just like Sir Christopher Wren. He had been concerned in an electric lighting business, and had been revolted by the prodigious number of breakages of glass bulbs involved by the handling of the crates in which they were packed for transport by rail and road. What was needed was a method of transferring the crates from truck to truck, and from truck to road lorry, and from road lorry to warehouse lift without shock, friction, or handling. Gattie, being, I suppose, by natural genius an inventor though by mistaken vocation a playwright, solved the mechanical problem without apparent difficulty, and offered his nation the means of effecting an enormous saving of labor and smash. But instead of being received with open arms as a social benefactor he found himself up against Breakages, Limited. The glass blowers whose employment was threatened, the exploiters of the great industry of repairing our railway trucks (every time a goods train is stopped a series of 150 violent collisions is propagated from end to end of the train, as those who live within earshot know to their cost), and the railway porters who dump the crates from truck to platform and then hurl them into other trucks, shattering bulbs, battering cans, and too often rupturing themselves in the process, saw in Gattie an enemy of the human race, a wrecker of homes and a starver of innocent babes. He fought them undauntedly; but they were too strong for him; and in due time his patents expired and he died almost unrecognized, whilst Unknown Soldiers were being canonized throughout the world. So far, The Apple Cart is his only shrine; and as it does not even bear his name, I have written it here pending its tardy appearance in the roll of fame.

I must not leave my readers to assume that Gattie was an easy man to deal with, or that he handled the opposition in a conciliatory manner with due allowance for the inertia of a somewhat unimaginative officialdom which had not, like myself, sat on his trucks, and probably set him down as a Utopian (a species much dreaded in Government departments) and thus missed the real point, which was that he was an inventor. Like many men of genius he could not understand why things obvious to him should not be so at once to other people, and found it easier to believe that they were corrupt than that they could be so stupid. Once, after I had urged him to be more diplomatic, he brought me, with some pride, a letter to the Board of Trade which he considered a masterpiece of tact and good temper. It contained not a word descriptive of his invention; and it began somewhat in this fashion: "Sir: If you are an honest man you cannot deny that among the worst abuses of this corrupt age is the acceptance of city directorships by retired members of the Board of Trade." Clearly it was not easy for the Board of Trade to deal with an inventor who wished to interest them, not in his new machines, but in the desirability of its abolishing itself as infamous.

The last time I saw him he called on me to unfold a new scheme of much greater importance, as he declared, than his trucks. He was very interesting on that occasion. He began by giving me a vivid account of the pirates who used to infest the Thames below London Bridge before the docks were built. He described how the docks had come into existence not as wharves for loading and unloading but as strongholds in which ships and their cargoes could be secure from piracy. They are now, he declared, a waste of fabulously valuable ground; and their work should be done in quite another way. He then produced plans of a pier to be built in the middle of the river, communicating directly by rail and road with the shore and the great main lines. The ships would come alongside the pier; and by a simple system of hoists the contents of their holds would be lifted out and transferred (like myself in the armchair) to railway trucks or motor lorries without being touched by a human hand and therefore without risk of breakage. It was all so masterly, so simple in its complexity, so convincing as to its practicability, and so prodigiously valuable socially, that I, taking it very seriously, proceeded to discuss what could be done to interest the proper people in it.

To my amazement Gattie began to shew unmistakeable signs of disappointment and indignation. "You do not seem to understand me," he said. "I have shewn you all this mechanical stuff merely by way of illustration. What I have come to consult you about is a great melodrama I am going to write, the scene of which will be the Pool of London in the seventeenth century among the pirates!"

What could I or anyone do with a man like that? He was naïvely surprised when I laughed; and he went away only half persuaded that his scheme for turning the docks into building land; expediting the Thames traffic; saving much dangerous and demoralizingly casual labor; and transfiguring the underpaid stevedore into a fullfed electrician, was stupendously more important than any ridiculous melodrama. He admitted that there was of course all that in it; but I could see that his heart was in the melodrama.

As it was evident that officialdom, writhing under his insults and shocked by his utter lack of veneration for bigwigs, besides being hampered as all our Government departments are by the vested interests of Breakages, Limited, would do nothing for him, I induced some less embarrassed public persons to take a ride in the trucks and be convinced that they really existed and worked. But here again the parallel between Gattie and his fellow-amateur Sir Christopher Wren came in. Wren was not content to redesign and rebuild St Paul's: he wanted to redesign London as well. He was quite right: what we have lost by not letting him do it is incalculable. Similarly, Gattie was not content to improve the luggage arrangements of our railways: he would not listen to you if your mind was not large enough to grasp the immediate necessity for a new central clearing house in Farringdon Market, connected with the existing railways by a system of new tubes. He was of course right; and we have already lost by sticking to our old ways more than the gigantic sum his scheme would have cost. But neither the money nor the enterprise was available just then, with the war on our hands. The Clearing House, like the Thames pier, remains on paper; and Gattie is in his grave. But I still hold that there must have been something great in a man who, having not only imagined them but invented their machinery, could, far from being crushed by their rejection, exclaim "Perish all my mechanical trash if only it provides material for one bad play!"

This little history will explain how it actually did provide material for Breakages, Limited, and for the bitter cry of the Powermistress General. Not until Breakages is itself broken will it cease to have a message for us.

Ayot St Lawrence
March 1930

CONTENTS

ACT I

An office in the royal palace. Two writing tables face each other from opposite sides of the room, leaving plenty of room between them. Each table has a chair by it for visitors. The door is in the middle of the farthest wall. The clock shews that it is a little past II; and the light is that of a fine summer morning.

Sempronius, smart and still presentably young, shews his right profile as he sits at one of the tables opening the King's letters. Pamphilius, middle aged, shews his left as he leans back in his chair at the other table with a pile of the morning papers at his elbow, reading one of them. This goes on silently for some time. Then Pamphilius, putting down his paper, looks at Sempronius for a moment before speaking.

PAMPHILIUS: What was your father?

SEMPRONIUS [*startled*] Eh?

PAMPHILIUS: What was your father?

SEMPRONIUS: My father?

PAMPHILIUS: Yes. What was he?

SEMPRONIUS: A Ritualist.

PAMPHILIUS: I dont mean his religion. I mean his profession. And his politics.

SEMPRONIUS: He was a Ritualist by profession, a Ritualist in politics, a Ritualist in religion: a raging emotional Die Hard Ritualist right down to his boots.

PAMPHILIUS: Do you mean that he was a parson?

SEMPRONIUS: Not at all. He was a sort of spectacular artist. He got up pageants and Lord Mayors' Shows and military tattoos and big public ceremonies and things like that. He arranged the last two coronations. That was how I got my job here in the palace. All our royal people knew him quite well: he was behind the scenes with them.

PAMPHILIUS: Behind the scenes and yet believed they were all real!

SEMPRONIUS: Yes. Believed in them with all his soul.

PAMPHILIUS: Although he manufactured them himself?

SEMPRONIUS: Certainly. Do you suppose a baker cannot believe sincerely in the sacrifice of the Mass or in holy communion because he has baked the consecrated wafer himself?

PAMPHILIUS: I never thought of that.

SEMPRONIUS: My father might have made millions in the theatres and film studios. But he refused to touch them because the things they represented hadnt really happened. He didnt mind doing the christening of Queen Elizabeth in Shakespear's Henry the Eighth because that had really happened. It was a celebration of royalty. But not anything romantic: not though they offered him thousands.

PAMPHILIUS: Did you ever ask him what he really thought about it all? But of course you didnt: one cant ask one's father anything about himself.

SEMPRONIUS: My dear Pam: my father never thought. He didnt know what thought meant. Very few people do, you know. He had vision: actual bodily vision, I mean; and he had an oddly limited sort of imagination. What I mean is that he couldnt imagine anything he didnt see; but he could imagine that what he did see was divine and holy and omniscient and omnipotent and eternal and everything that is impossible if only it looked splendid enough, and the organ was solemn enough, or the military bands brassy enough.

PAMPHILIUS: You mean that he had to get everything from outside.

SEMPRONIUS: Exactly. He'd never have felt anything if he hadnt had parents to feel about in his childhood, and a wife and babies to feel about when he grew up. He'd never have known anything if he hadn't been taught at school. He couldnt amuse himself: he had to pay oceans of money to other people to amuse him with all sorts of ghastly sports and pleasures that would have driven me into a monastery to escape from them. You see it was all ritual: he went to the Riviera every winter just as he went to church.

PAMPHILIUS: By the way, is he alive? I should like to know him.

SEMPRONIUS: No. He died in 1962, of solitude.

PAMPHILIUS: What do you mean? of solitude?

SEMPRONIUS: He couldnt bear to be alone for a moment: it was death to him. Somebody had to be with him always.

PAMPHILIUS: Oh well, come! That was friendly and kindly. It shews he had something inside him after all.

SEMPRONIUS: Not a bit. He never talked to his friends. He played cards with them. They never exchanged a thought.

PAMPHILIUS: He must have been a rum old bird.

SEMPRONIUS: Not rum enough to be noticed. There are millions like him.

PAMPHILIUS: But what about his dying of solitude? Was he imprisoned?

SEMPRONIUS: No. His yacht struck a reef and sank somewhere off the north of Scotland; and he managed to swim to an uninhabited island. All the rest were drowned; and he was not taken off for three weeks. When they found him he was melancholy mad, poor old boy; and he never got over it. Simply from having no one to play cards with, and no church to go to.

PAMPHILIUS: My dear Sem: one isnt alone on an uninhabited island. My mother used to stand me on the table and make me recite about it.

[*He declaims*]

> To sit on rocks; to muse o'er flood and fell;
> To slowly trace the forest's shady scene
> Where things that own not man's dominion dwell
> And mortal foot hath ne'er or rarely been;
> To climb the trackless mountain all unseen
> With the wild flock that never needs a fold;
> Alone o'er steeps and foaming falls to lean:
> This is not solitude: 'tis but to hold
> Converse with Nature's charms, and view her stores unrolled.

SEMPRONIUS: Now you have hit the really funny thing about my father. All that about the lonely woods and the rest of it—what you call Nature—didnt exist for him. It had to be something artificial to get at him. Nature to him meant nakedness; and nakedness only disgusted him. He wouldnt look at a horse grazing in a field; but put splendid trappings on it and stick it into a procession and he just loved it. The same with men and women: they were nothing to him until they were dressed up in fancy costumes and painted and wigged and titled. To him the sacredness of the priest was the beauty of his vestment, the loveliness of women the dazzle of their jewels and robes, the charm of the countryside not in its hills and trees, nor in the blue smoke from its cottages in the winter evenings, but of its temples, palaces, mansions, park gates, and porticoed country houses. Think of the horror of that island to him! A void! a place where he was deaf and dumb and blind and lonely! If only there had been a peacock with its tail in full bloom it might have saved his reason; but all the birds were gulls; and gulls are not decorative. Our King could have lived there for thirty years with nothing but his own thoughts. You would have been all right with a fishing rod and a golf ball with a bag of clubs. I should have been as happy as a man in a picture gallery looking at the dawns and sunsets, the changing seasons, the continual miracle of life ever renewing itself. Who could be dull with pools in the rocks to watch? Yet my father, with all that under his nose, was driven mad by its nothingness. They say that where there is nothing the king loses his rights. My father found that where there is nothing a man loses his reason and dies.

PAMPHILIUS: Let me add that in this palace, when the king's letters are not ready for him at 12 o'clock, a secretary loses his job.

SEMPRONIUS [*hastily resuming his work*] Yes, devil take you: why did you start me talking before I had finished my work? You have nothing to do but pretend to read the newspapers for him; and when you say 'Nothing particular this morning, Sir,' all he says is 'Thank Heaven!' But if I missed a note from one of his aunts inviting herself to tea, or a little line from Orinthia the Beloved marked 'Strictly private and confidential: to be opened by His Majesty alone,' I should never hear the end of it. He had six love letters yesterday; and all he said when I told him was 'Take them to The Queen.' He thinks they amuse her. I believe they make her as sick as they make me.

PAMPHILIUS: Do Orinthia's letters go to The Queen?

SEMPRONIUS: No, by George! Even I dont read Orinthia's letters. My instructions are to read everything; but I take care to forget to open hers. And I notice that I am not rebuked for my negligence.

PAMPHILIUS [*thoughtfully*] I suppose—

SEMPRONIUS: Oh shut up, Pam. I shall never get through if you go on talking.

PAMPHILIUS: I was only going to say that I suppose—

SEMPRONIUS: Something about Orinthia. Dont. If you indulge in supposition on that subject, you will lose your job, old chap. So stow it.

PAMPHILIUS: Dont cry out before Orinthia is hurt, young chap. I was going to say that I suppose you know that that bull-roarer Boanerges has just been taken into the Cabinet as President of the Board of Trade, and that he is coming here today to give the King a piece of his mind, or what he calls his mind, about the crisis.

SEMPRONIUS: What does the King care about the crisis? There has been a crisis every two months since he came to the throne; but he has always been too clever for them. He'll turn Boanerges inside out after letting him roar the palace down.

Boanerges enters, dressed in a Russian blouse and peaked cap, which he keeps on. He is fifty, heavily built and aggressively self-assertive.

BOANERGES: Look here. The King has an appointment with me at a quarter to twelve. How long more am I to be kept waiting?

SEMPRONIUS [*with cheerful politeness*] Good morning. Mr Boanerges, I think.

BOANERGES [*shortly, but a little taken aback*] Oh, good morning to you. They say that politeness is the punctuality of kings—

SEMPRONIUS: The other way about, Mr Boanerges. Punctuality is the politeness of kings; and King Magnus is a model in that respect. Your arrival cannot have been announced to His Majesty. I will see about it. [*He hurries out*].

PAMPHILIUS: Be seated, Mr Boanerges.

BOANERGES [*seating himself by Pamphilius's writing-table*] A nice lot of young upstarts you have in this palace, Mr—?

PAMPHILIUS: Pamphilius is my name.

BOANERGES: Oh yes: Ive heard of you. Youre one of the king's private secretaries.

PAMPHILIUS: I am. And what have our young upstarts been doing to you, Mr Boanerges?

BOANERGES: Well, I told one of them to tell the king I was here, and to look sharp about it. He looked at me as if I was a performing elephant, and took himself off after whispering to another flunkey. Then this other chap comes over to me and pretends he doesnt know who I am! asks me can he have my name! 'My lad' I said: 'not to know me argues yourself unknown. You know who I am as well as I do myself. Go and tell the king I'm waiting for him, d'ye see?' So he took himself off with a flea in his ear. I waited until I was fed up with it, and then opened the nearest door and came in here.

PAMPHILIUS: Young rascals! However, my friend Mr Sempronius will make it all right for you.

BOANERGES: Oh: that was Sempronius, was it. Ive heard of him too.

PAMPHILIUS: You seem to have heard of all of us. You will be quite at home in the palace now that you are a Cabinet Minister. By the way, may I congratulate you on your appointment—or rather congratulate the Cabinet on your accession?

SEMPRONIUS [*returning*] The King. [*He goes to his table and takes the visitor's chair in his hand, ready for the king's instructions as to where to place it*].

Pamphilius rises. Boanerges turns to the door in his chair without rising. King Magnus, a tallish studious looking gentleman of 45 or thereabouts, enters, and comes quickly down the middle of the room to Boanerges, proffering his hand cordially.

MAGNUS: You are very welcome to my little palace, Mr BOANERGES. Wont you sit down?

BOANERGES: I am sitting down.

MAGNUS: True, Mr Boanerges. I had not noticed it. Forgive me: force of habit.

He indicates to Sempronius that he wishes to sit near Boanerges, on his right. Sempronius places the chair accordingly.

MAGNUS: You will allow me to be seated?

BOANERGES: Oh, sit down, man, sit down. Youre in your own house: ceremony cuts no ice with me.

MAGNUS [*gratefully*] Thank you.

The King sits. Pamphilius sits. Sempronius returns to his table and sits.

MAGNUS: It is a great pleasure to meet you at last, Mr Boanerges. I have followed your career with interest ever since you contested Northampton twenty-five years ago.

BOANERGES [*pleased and credulous*] I should just think you have, King Magnus. I have made you sit up once or twice, eh?

MAGNUS [*smiling*] Your voice has shaken the throne oftener than that.

BOANERGES [*indicating the secretaries with a jerk of his head*] What about these two? Are they to overhear everything that passes?

MAGNUS: My private secretaries. Do they incommode you?

BOANERGES: Oh, they dont incommode me. I am ready to have our talk out in Trafalgar Square if you like, or have it broadcast on the wireless.

MAGNUS: That would be a treat for my people, Mr Boanerges. I am sorry we have not arranged for it.

BOANERGES [*gathering himself together formidably*] Yes; but do you realize that I am going to say things to you that have never been said to a king before?

MAGNUS: I am very glad indeed to hear it, Mr Boanerges. I thought I had already heard everything that could possible be said to a king. I shall be grateful for the smallest novelty.

BOANERGES: I warn you it wont be agreeable. I am a plain man, Magnus: a very plain man.

MAGNUS: Not at all, I assure you—

BOANERGES [*indignantly*] I was not alluding to my personal appearance.

MAGNUS [*gravely*] Nor was I. Do not deceive yourself, Mr Boanerges. You are very far from being a plain man. To me you have always been an Enigma.

BOANERGES [*surprised and enormously flattered; he cannot help smiling with pleasure*] Well, perhaps I am a bit of an enigma. Perhaps I am.

MAGNUS [*humbly*] I wish I could see through you, Mr Boanerges. But I have not your sort of cleverness. I can only ask you to be frank with me.

BOANERGES [*now convinced that he has the upper hand*] You mean about the crisis. Well, frank is just what I have come here to be. And the first thing I am going to tell you frankly about it is that this country has got to be governed, not by you, but by your ministers.

MAGNUS: I shall be only too grateful to them for taking a very difficult and thankless job off my hands.

BOANERGES: But it's not on your hands. It's on your ministers' hands. You are only a constitutional monarch. Do you know what they call that in Belgium?

MAGNUS: An indiarubber stamp, I think. Am I right?

BOANERGES: You are, King Magnus. An indiarubber stamp. Thats what you have got to be; and dont you forget it.

MAGNUS: Yes: thats what we are most of the time: both of us.

BOANERGES [*outraged*] What do you mean? both of us?

MAGNUS: They bring us papers. We sign. You have no time to read them, luckily for you. But I am expected to read everything. I do not always agree; but I must sign: there is nothing else to be done. For instance, death warrants. Not only have I to sign the death warrants of persons who in my opinion ought not to be killed; but I may not even issue death warrants for a great many people who in my opinion ought to be killed.

BOANERGES [*sarcastic*] Youd like to be able to say "Off with his head!" wouldnt you?

MAGNUS: Many men would hardly miss their heads, there is so little in them. Still, killing is a serious business: at least the person who is to be killed is usually conceited enough to think so. I think that if there were a question of killing me—

BOANERGES [*grimly*] There may be, someday. I have heard it discussed.

MAGNUS: Oh, quite. I have not forgotten King Charles's head. Well, I hope it will be settled by a living person and not by an indiarubber stamp.

BOANERGES: It will be settled by the Home Secretary, your duly constituted democratic minister.

MAGNUS: Another indiarubber stamp, eh?

BOANERGES: At present, perhaps. But not when I am Home Secretary, by Jingo! Nobody will make an indiarubber stamp of Bill Boanerges: take that from me.

MAGNUS: Of course not. Is it not curious how people idealize their rulers? In the old days the king—poor man!—was a god, and was actually called God and worshipped as infallible and omniscient. That was monstrous—

BOANERGES: It was silly: just silly.

MAGNUS: But was it half so silly as our pretence that he is an indiarubber stamp? The ancient Roman emperor-god had not infinite wisdom, infinite knowledge, infinite power; but he had some: perhaps even as much as his ministers. He was alive, not dead. What man has ever approached either a king or a minister and been able to pick him up from the table and use him as one picks up and uses a piece of wood and brass and rubber? Permanent officials of your department will try to pick you up and use you like that. Nineteen times out of twenty you will have to let them do it, because you cannot know everything; and even if you could you cannot do everything and be everywhere. But what about the twentieth time?

BOANERGES: The twentieth time they will find they are up against Bill Boanerges, eh?

MAGNUS: Precisely. The indiarubber stamp theory will not work, Mr. Boanerges: The old divine theory worked because there is a divine spark in us all; and the stupidest or worst monarch or minister, if not wholly god, is a bit of a god—an attempt at a god—however little the bit and unsuccessful the attempt. But the indiarubber stamp theory breaks down in every real emergency, because no king or minister is the very least little bit like a stamp: he is a living soul.

BOANERGES: A soul, eh? You kings still believe in that, I suppose.

MAGNUS: I find the word convenient: it is short and familiar. But if you dislike being called a soul, let us say that you are animate matter as distinguished from inanimate.

BOANERGES [*not quite liking this*] I think I'd rather you called me a soul, you know, if you must call me anything at all. I know I have too much matter about me: the doctor says I ought to knock off a stone or two; but there's something more to me than beef. Call it a soul if you like; only not in a superstitious sense, if you understand me.

MAGNUS: Perfectly. So you see, Mr Boanerges, that though we have been dealing with one another for less than ten minutes, you have already led me into an intellectual discussion which shews that we are something more than a pair of indiarubber stamps. You are up against my brains, such as they are.

BOANERGES: And you are up against mine.

MAGNUS [*gallantly*] There can be no doubt of that.

BOANERGES [*grinning*] Such as they are, eh?

MAGNUS: It is not for me to make that qualification, except in my own case. Besides, you have given your proofs. No common man could have risen as you have done. As for me, I am a king because I was the nephew of my uncle, and because my two elder brothers died. If I had been the stupidest man in the country I should still be its king. I have not won my position by my merits. If I had been born as you were in the—in the—

BOANERGES: In the gutter. Out with it. Picked up by a policeman at the foot of Captain Coram's statue. Adopted by the policeman's grandmother, bless her!

MAGNUS: Where should *I* have been if the policeman had picked me up?

BOANERGES: Ah! Where? Not, mind you, that you mightnt have done pretty well for yourself. Youre no fool, Magnus: I will say that for you.

MAGNUS: You flatter me.

BOANERGES: Flatter a king! Never. Not Bill Boanerges.

MAGNUS: Yes, yes: everybody flatters the King. But everybody has not your tact, and, may I say? your good nature.

BOANERGES [*beaming with self-satisfaction*] Perhaps not. Still, I am a Republican, you know.

MAGNUS: That is what has always surprised me. Do you really think that any man should have as much personal power as the presidents of the republican States have? Ambitious kings envy them.

BOANERGES: What's that? I dont follow that.

MAGNUS [*smiling*] You cannot humbug me, Mr Boanerges. I see why you are a Republican. If the English people send me packing and establish a republic, no man has a better chance of being the first British president than you.

BOANERGES [*almost blushing*] Oh! I dont say that.

MAGNUS: Come come! You know it as well as I do. Well, if it happens you will have ten times more power than I have ever had.

BOANERGES [*not quite convinced*] How can that be? Youre King.

MAGNUS: And what is the King? An idol set up by a group of plutocrats so that they can rule the country with the King as their scapegoat and puppet. Presidents, now, are chosen by the people, who always want a Strong Man to protect them against the rich.

BOANERGES: Well, speaking as a bit of a Strong Man myself, there may be something in that. But honestly, Magnus, as man to man, do you tell me youd rather be a president than what you are?

MAGNUS: By no means. You wouldnt believe me if I did; and you would be quite right. You see, my security is very comfortable.

BOANERGES: Security, eh? You admitted just now that even a modest individual like myself had given your throne a shake or two.

MAGNUS: True. You are quite right to remind me of it. I know that the monarchy may come to an end at any moment. But while the monarchy lasts—while it lasts, mark you—I am very secure. I escape the dreadful and demoralizing drudgery of electioneering. I have no voters to please. Ministers come and ministers go; but I go on for ever. The terrible precariousness of your position—

BOANERGES: What's that? How is my position precarious?

MAGNUS: The vote may go against you. Yours is a Trade Union seat, is it not? If the Hydro-Electric Workers Federation throw you over, where would you be?

BOANERGES [*confidently*] They wont throw me over. You dont know the workers, Magnus: you have never been a worker.

MAGNUS [*lifts his eyebrows*]!

BOANERGES [*continuing*] No king on earth is as safe in his job as a Trade Union Official. There is only one thing that can get him sacked; and that is drink. Not even that, as long as he doesnt actually fall down. I talk democracy to these men and women. I tell them that they have the vote, and that theirs is the kingdom and the power and the glory. I say to them 'You are supreme: exercise your power.' They say, 'That's right: tell us what to do'; and I tell them. I say 'Exercise your vote intelligently by voting for me.' And they do. That's democracy; and a splendid thing it is too for putting the right men in the right place.

MAGNUS: Magnificent! I have never heard it better described. You certainly have a head on you, Mr Boanerges. You should write an essay on democracy. But—

BOANERGES: But what?

MAGNUS: Suppose a man with a bigger voice comes along! Some fool! Some windbag! Some upstart with a platform trick of gulling the multitude!

BOANERGES: Youre thinking of Iky Jacobus? He is only a talker. [*Snapping his fingers*] I dont give that for him.

MAGNUS: I never even heard of Mr Jacobus. But why do you say 'only a talker.' Talkers are very formidable rivals for popular favor. The multitude understands talk: it does not understand work. I mean brain work, like yours and mine.

BOANERGES: That's true. But I can talk Iky's head off.

MAGNUS: Lucky man: you have all the trumps in your hand. But I, who cannot pretend to your gifts, am very glad that Iky cannot upset me as long as I am the nephew of my uncle.

A young lady, dressed for walking, rushes in impetuously.

THE YOUNG LADY: Papa: I cannot find the address—

MAGNUS [*cutting her short*] No, no, no, dear: not now. Go away. Dont you see that I am particularly engaged with the President of the Board of Trade? You must excuse my unruly daughter, Mr. Boanerges: May I present her to you? Alice, my eldest girl. Mr. Boanerges, dear.

Alice: Oh! Are you the great Mr. Boanerges?

BOANERGES [*rising in a glow of gratification*] Well, I dont call myself that, you know. But I believe the expression is in use, as you might say. I am very pleased indeed to make the acquaintance of the Princess Royal.

They shake hands.

ALICE: Why do you wear such awful clothes, Mr. Boanerges?

MAGNUS [*remonstrating*] My dear—!

ALICE [*continuing*] I cant go out walking with you in that [*pointing to his blouse*].

BOANERGES: The uniform of Labor, your Royal Highness. I'm proud of it.

ALICE: Oh yes, I know all that, Mr. Boanerges. But you dont look the part, you know. Anyone can see that you belong naturally to the governing class.

BOANERGES [*struck by this view*] In a way, perhaps. But I have earned my bread by my hands. Not as a laborer, though. I am a skilled mechanic, or was until my country called on me to lead it.

MAGNUS [*to Alice*] Well, my dear, you have broken up a most interesting conversation, and to me a most instructive one. It's no use our trying to go on, Mr. Boanerges: I must go and find what my daughter wants, though I strongly suspect that what she really came in for was to see my wonderful new minister. We shall meet again presently: you know that the Prime Minister is calling on me today with some of his colleagues—including, I hope, yourself—to discuss the crisis. [*Taking Alice's arm and turning towards the door*] You will excuse us, wont you?

BOANERGES [*graciously*] Oh, thats all right. Thats quite all right.

The King and the Princess go out, apparently much pleased.

BOANERGES [*to Sempronius and Pamphilius comprehensively*] Well, say what you will, the King is no fool. Not when you know how to handle him.

PAMPHILIUS: Of course, that makes all the difference.

BOANERGES: And the girl hasnt been spoilt. I was glad to see that. She doesnt seem to know that she is the Princess Royal, eh?

SEMPRONIUS: Well, she wouldnt dream of giving herself any airs with you.

BOANERGES: What! Isnt she always like that?

SEMPRONIUS: Oh no. It's not everybody who is received as you have been. I hope you have enjoyed your visit.

BOANERGES: Well, I pulled Magnus through it pretty well: eh? Dont you think so?

SEMPRONIUS: He was pleased. You have a way with him, Mr. President.

BOANERGES: Well, perhaps I have, perhaps I have.

A bevy of five Cabinet Ministers, resplendent in diplomatic uniforms, enters. Proteus the Prime Minister has on his left, Pliny, Chancellor of the Exchequer, good-humored and conciliatory, and Nicobar, Foreign Secretary, snaky and censorious. On his right Crassus, Colonial Secretary, elderly and anxious, and Balbus, Home Secretary, rude and thoughtless.

BALBUS: Holy snakes! look at Bill. [*To Boanerges*] Go home and dress yourself properly, man.

NICOBAR: Where do you think you are?

CRASSUS: Who do you think you are?

PLINY [*fingering the blouse*] Where did you buy it, Bill?

BOANERGES [*turning on them like a baited bear*] Well, if you come to that, who do you think you are, the lot of you?

PROTEUS [*conciliatory*] Never mind them, Bill: theyre jealous because they didnt think of it themselves. How did you get on with the King?

BOANERGES: Right as rain, Joe. You leave the King to me. I know how to handle him. If I'd been in the Cabinet these last three months there'd have been no crisis.

NICOBAR: He put you through it, did he?

BOANERGES: What do you mean? put me through it? Is this a police office?

PLINY: The third degree is not unknown in this palace my boy. [*To Pamphilius*] Did the matron take a hand?

PAMPHILIUS: No. But the Princess Alice happened to drop in. She was greatly impressed by the President.

They all laugh uproariously at Boanerges.

BOANERGES: What in hell are you laughing at?

PROTEUS: Take no notice of them, Bill: they are only having their bit of fun with you as a new comer. Come, lads! enough of fooling: lets get to business. [*He takes the chair vacated by the King*].

Sempronius and Pamphilius at once rise and go out busily, taking some of their papers with them. Pliny takes Boanerges' chair, Balbus that of Sempronius, Boanerges that of Pamphilius, whilst Nicobar and Crassus take chairs from the wall and sit down at the ends of the writing tables, left and right of the Prime Minister respectively.

PROTEUS: Now to start with, do you chaps all fully realize that though we wiped out every other party at the last election, and have been in power for the last three years, this country has been governed during that time by the King?

NICOBAR: I dont see that. We—

PROTEUS [*impatiently*] Well, if you don't, then for Heaven's sake either resign and get out of the way of men who can see facts and look them in the face, or else take my job and lead the party yourself.

NICOBAR: The worst of you is that you wont face the fact that though youre Prime Minister youre not God Almighty. The king cant do anything except what we advise him to do. How can he govern the country if we have all the power and he has none?

BOANERGES: Dont talk silly, Nick. This indiarubber stamp theory doesn't work. What man has ever approached a king or a minister and been able to pick him up from the table and use him as youd use a bit of wood and brass and rubber? The King's a live man; and what more are you, with your blessed advice?

PLINY: Hullo, Bill! You have been having your mind improved by somebody.

BOANERGES: What do you mean? Isnt it what I have always said?

PROTEUS [*whose nerves are on edge*] Oh, will you stop squabbling. What are we going to say to the King when he comes in? If you will only hold together and say the same thing—or let me say it—he must give way. But he is as artful as the very devil. He'll have a pin to stick into the seat of every man of you. If you all start quarrelling and scolding and bawling, which is just what he wants you to do, it will end in his having his own way as usual, because one man that has a mind and knows it can always beat ten men who havnt and dont.

PLINY: Steady, Prime Minister. Youre overwrought.

PROTEUS: It's enough to drive a man mad. I am sorry.

PLINY [*changing the subject*] Where's Mandy?

NICOBAR: And Lizzie?

PROTEUS: Late as usual. Come! Business, business, business.

BOANERGES [*thunderously*] Order order!

PROTEUS: The King is working the Press against us. The King is making speeches. Things have come to a head. He said yesterday on the opening of the new Chamber of Commerce building that the king's veto is the only remaining defence of the people against corrupt legislation.

BOANERGES: So it is, by Jingo. What other defence is there? Democracy? Yah! We know what Democracy is worth. What we need is a Strong Man.

NICOBAR [*sneering*] Yourself for instance.

BOANERGES: I should stand a better chance than you, my lad, if we were a Republic, and the people could choose. And let me tell you that a republican president has more power than a king because the people know that they need a Strong Man to protect them against the rich.

PROTEUS [*flinging himself back in his chair in desperation*] This is a nice thing. Two Labor papers have leading articles this morning supporting the King; and the latest addition to the Cabinet here is a King's man. I resign.

General consternation except on the part of Nicobar, who displays cheerful unconcern, and of Boanerges, who squares himself with an iron face.

PLINY: } No: dont do that, Joe.
BALBUS: } What! Now! You cant. You mustnt.
CRASSUS: } Of course not. Out of the question.

PROTEUS: No use. [*Rising*] I resign, I tell you. You can all go to the devil. I have lost my health, and almost lost my reason, trying to keep this Cabinet together in the face of the cunningest enemy popular government has ever had to face. I have had enough of it. [*Sitting down again*] I resign.

CRASSUS: But not at such a moment as this. Dont let us swop horses when crossing a stream.

NICOBAR: Why not, if the horse you have got is subject to hysterics?

BOANERGES: Not to mention that you may have more than one horse at your disposal.

PROTEUS: Right you are. Perfectly true. Take my job, Nick. It's vacant for you, Bill. I wish you joy of it.

PLINY: Now boys, boys, boys: be good. We cant make a new Cabinet before Magnus comes in. You have something in your pocket, Joe. Out with it. Read it to them.

PROTEUS [*taking a paper from his pocket*] What I was going to propose—and you can take it or leave it—is an ultimatum.

CRASSUS: Good!

PROTEUS: Either he signs this, or — [*he pauses significantly*]—!

NICOBAR: Or what?

PROTEUS [*disgusted*] Oh, you make me sick.

NICOBAR: Youre sick already, by your own account. I only ask, suppose he refuses to sign your ultimatum?

PROTEUS: You call yourself a Cabinet Minister, and you cant answer that!

NICOBAR: No I cant. I press my question. You said he must sign, OR. I ask, or what?

PROTEUS: Or we resign and tell the country that we cant carry on the King's Government under conditions which destroy our responsibility.

BALBUS: Thatll do it. He couldnt face that.

CRASSUS: Yes: thatll bunker him.

PROTEUS: Is that agreed?

PLINY: } Yes, yes, yes, 'greed' greed' greed.
CRASSUS:
BALBUS:

BOANERGES: I retain an open mind. Let us hear the ultimatum.

NICOBAR: Yes: lets hear it.

PROTEUS: Memorandum of understanding arrived at—

The King enters, with Amanda, Postmistress General, a merry lady in uniform like the men, on his left, and Lysistrata, Powermistress General, a grave lady in academic robes, on his right. All rise. The Prime Minister's face darkens.

MAGNUS: Welcome, gentlemen. I hope I am not too early. [*Noting the Prime Minister's scowl*] Am I intruding?

PROTEUS: I protest. It is intolerable. I call a conference of my Cabinet to consider our position in regard to the prerogative; and I find the two lady members, the Postmistress General and the Powermistress General, closeted with your Majesty instead of being in their places to confer with me.

LYSISTRATA: You mind your own business, Joe.

MAGNUS: Oh no: really, really, my dear Lysistrata, you must not take that line. Our business is to meddle in everybody's business. A Prime Minister is a busybody by profession. So is a monarch. So are we all.

LYSISTRATA: Well, they say everybody's business is nobody's business, which is just what Joe is fit for. [*She takes a chair from the wall with a powerful hand, and swings it forward to the inside corner of Sempronius's table, where she stands waiting for the King to sit down.*]

PROTEUS: This is what I have to put up with when I am on the verge of a nervous breakdown [*he sits down distractedly, and buries his face in his hands*].

AMANDA [*going to him and petting him*] Come, Joe! dont make a scene. You asked for it, you know.

NICOBAR: What do you go provoking Lizzie for like that? You know she has a temper.

LYSISTRATA: There is nothing whatever wrong with my temper. But I am not going to stand any of Joe's nonsense; and the sooner he makes up his mind to that the smoother our proceedings are likely to be.

BOANERGES: I protest. I say, let us be dignified. I say, let us respect ourselves and respect the throne. All this Joe and Bill and Nick and Lizzie: we might as well be hobnobbing in a fried fish shop. The Prime Minister is the prime minister: he isnt Joe. The Powermistress isnt Lizzie: she's Lysis Traitor.

LYSISTRATA [*who has evidently been a schoolmistress*] Certainly not, Bill. She is Ly Sistrata. You had better say Lizzie: it is easier to pronounce.

BOANERGES [*scornfully*] Ly Sistrata! A more foolish affectation I never heard: you might as well call me Bo Annerjeeze [*he flings himself into his chair*].

MAGNUS [*sweetly*] Shall we sit, ladies and gentlemen!

Boanerges hastily rises and sits down again. The King sits in Pliny's chair. Lysistrata and the rest of the men resume their seats, leaving Pliny and Amanda standing. Amanda takes an empty chair in each hand and plants them side by side between the King and the table of Pamphilius.

AMANDA: There you are, Plin. [*She sits next the table*].

PLINY: Ta ta, Mandy. Pardon me: I should have said AMANDA: [*He sits next the King*].

AMANDA: Dont mention it, darling.

BOANERGES: Order, order!

AMANDA [*waves him a kiss*]!!

MAGNUS: Prime Minister: the word is with you. Why have you all simultaneously given me the great pleasure of exercising your constitutional right of access to the sovereign?

LYSISTRATA: Have I that right, sir; or havnt I?

MAGNUS: Most undoubtedly you have.

LYSISTRATA: You hear that, Joe?

PROTEUS: I—

BALBUS: Oh for Heaven's sake dont contradict her, Joe. We shall never get anywhere at this rate. Come to the crisis.

NICOBAR:		Yes yes: the crisis!
CRASSUS:	[*together*]	Yes yes: come along!
PLINY:		The crisis: out with it!

BALBUS: The ultimatum. Lets have the ultimatum.

MAGNUS: Oh, there is an ultimatum! I gathered from yesterday's evening papers that there is a crisis—another crisis. But the ultimatum is new to me. [*To Proteus*] Have you an ultimatum?

PROTEUS: Your Majesty's allusion to the royal veto in a speech yesterday has brought matters to a head.

MAGNUS: It was perhaps indelicate. But you all allude so freely to your own powers—to the supremacy of Parliament and the voice of the people and so forth—that I fear I have lost any little delicacy I ever possessed. If you may flourish your thunderbolts why may I not shoulder my little popgun of a veto and strut up and down with it for a moment?

NICOBAR: This is not a subject for jesting—

MAGNUS [*interrupting him quickly*] I am not jesting, Mr. Nicobar. But I am certainly trying to discuss our differences in a good humored manner. Do you wish me to lose my temper and make scenes?

AMANDA: Oh please no, your Majesty. We get enough of that from Joe.

PROTEUS: I pro—

MAGNUS [*his hand persuasively on the Prime Minister's arm*] Take care, Prime Minister: take care: do not let your wily Postmistress General provoke you to supply the evidence against yourself.

All the rest laugh.

PROTEUS [*coolly*] I thank your Majesty for the caution. The Postmistress General has never forgiven me for not making her First Lady of the Admiralty. She has three nephews in the navy.

AMANDA: Oh you—[*She swallows the epithet, and contents herself with shaking her fist at the Premier*].

MAGNUS: Tch-tch-tch! Gently, Amanda, gently. Three very promising lads: they do you credit.

AMANDA: I never wanted them to go to sea. I could have found them better jobs in the Post Office.

MAGNUS: Apart from Amanda's family relations, am I face to face with a united Cabinet.

PLINY: No, sir. You are face to face with a squabbling Cabinet; but, on the constitutional question, united we stand: divided we fall.

BALBUS: That is so.

NICOBAR: Hear hear!

MAGNUS: What is the constitutional question? Do you deny the royal veto? or do you object only to my reminding my subjects of its existence?

NICOBAR: What we say is that the king has no right to remind his subjects of anything constitutional except by the advice of the Prime Minister, and in words which he has read and approved.

MAGNUS: Which Prime Minister? There are so many of them in the Cabinet.

BOANERGES: There! Serves you all right! Arnt you ashamed of yourselves? But I am not surprised, Joseph Proteus. I own I like a Prime Minister that knows how to be a Prime Minister. Why do you let them take the word out of your mouth every time?

PROTEUS: If His Majesty wants a Cabinet of dumb dogs he will not get it from my party.

BALBUS: Hear, hear, Joe!

MAGNUS: Heaven forbid! The variety of opinion in the Cabinet is always most instructive and interesting. Who is to be its spokesman today?

PROTEUS: I know your Majesty's opinion of me; but let—

MAGNUS [*before he can proceed*] Let me state it quite frankly. My opinion of you is that no man knows better than you when to speak and when to let others speak for you; when to make scenes and threaten resignation; and when to be as cool as a cucumber.

PROTEUS [*not altogether displeased*] Well, sir, I hope I am not such a fool as some fools think me. I may not always keep my temper. You would not be surprised at that if you knew how much temper I have to keep. [*He straightens up and becomes impressively eloquent*]. At this moment my cue is to shew you, not my own temper, but the temper of my Cabinet. What the Foreign Secretary and the Chancellor of the Exchequer and the Home Secretary have told you is true. If we are to carry on your government we cannot have you making speeches that express your own opinions and not ours. We cannot have you implying that everything that is of any value in our legislation is your doing and not ours. We cannot have you telling people that their only safeguard against the political encroachments of big business whilst we are doing nothing but bungling and squabbling is your power of veto. It has got to stop, once for all.

BALBUS: } Hear hear!
NICOBAR:

PROTEUS: Is that clear?

MAGNUS: Far clearer than I have ever dared to make it, Mr. Proteus. Except, by the way, on one point. When you say that all this of which you complain must cease once for all, do you mean that henceforth I am to agree with you or you with me?

PROTEUS: I mean that when you disagree with us you are to keep your disagreement to yourself.

MAGNUS: That would be a very heavy responsibility for me. If I see you leading the nation over the edge of a precipice may I not warn it?

BALBUS: It is our business to warn it, not yours.

MAGNUS: Suppose you dont do your business! Suppose you dont see the danger! That has happened. It may happen again.

CRASSUS [*insinuating*] As democrats, I think we are bound to proceed on the assumption that such a thing cannot happen.

BOANERGES: Rot! It's happening all the time until somebody has the gumption to put his foot down and stop it.

CRASSUS: Yes: I know. But that is not democracy.

BOANERGES: Democracy be—[*he leaves the word unspoken*]! I have thirty years experience of democracy. So have most of you. I say no more.

BALBUS: Wages are too high, if you ask me. Anybody can earn from five to twenty pounds a week now, and a big dole when there is no job for him. And what Englishman will give his mind to politics as long as he can afford to keep a motor car?

NICOBAR: How many voted at the last election? Not seven per cent of the register.

BALBUS: Yes; and the seven per cent were only a parcel of sillies playing at ins and outs. To make democracy work in Crassus's way we need poverty and hardship.

PROTEUS [*emphatically*] And we have abolished poverty and hardship. That is why the people trust us. [*To the King*] And that is why you will have to give way to us. We have the people of England in comfort—solid middle class comfort—at our backs.

MAGNUS: No: we have not abolished poverty and hardship. Our big business men have abolished them. But how? By sending our capital abroad to places where poverty and hardship still exist: in other words, where labor is cheap. We live in comfort on the imported profits of that capital. We are all ladies and gentlemen now.

NICOBAR: Well, what more do you want?

PLINY: You surely dont grudge us our wonderful prosperity, sir.

MAGNUS: I want it to last.

NICOBAR: Why shouldnt it last? [*Rising*] Own the truth. You had rather have the people poor, and pose as their champion and savior, than have to admit that the people are better off under our government—under our squabbling and bungling, as you call it.

MAGNUS: No: it was the Prime Minister who used those expressions.

NICOBAR: Dont quibble: he was quoting them from your reptile press. What I say is that we stand for high wages, and you are always belittling and opposing the men that pay them. Well, the voters like high wages. They know when they are well off; and they dont know what you are grumbling about; and thats what will beat you every time you try to stir them against us [*he resumes his seat*].

PLINY: There is no need to rub it in like that, Nick. We're all good friends. Nobody objects to prosperity.

MAGNUS: You think this prosperity is safe?

NICOBAR: Safe!

PLINY: Oh come, sir! Really!

BALBUS: Safe! Look at my constituency: Northeast-by-north Birmingham, with its four square miles of confectionery works! Do you know that in the Christmas cracker trade Birmingham is the workshop of the world?

CRASSUS: Take Gateshead and Middlesbrough alone! Do you know that there has not been a day's unemployment there for five years past, and that their daily output of chocolate creams totals up to twenty thousand tons?

MAGNUS: It is certainly a consoling thought that if we were peacefully blockaded by the League of Nations we could live for at least three weeks on our chocolate creams.

NICOBAR: You neednt sneer at the sweets: we turn out plenty of solid stuff. Where will you find the equal of the English golf club?

BALBUS: Look at the potteries: the new crown Derby! the new Chelsea! Look at the tapestries! Why, Greenwich Goblin has chased the French stuff out of the market.

CRASSUS: Dont forget our racing motor boats and cars, sir: the finest on earth, and all individually designed. No cheap mass production stuff there.

PLINY: And our live stock! Can you beat the English polo pony?

AMANDA: Or the English parlormaid? She wins in all the international beauty shows.

PLINY: Now Mandy, Mandy! None of your triviality.

MAGNUS: I am not sure that the British parlormaid is not the only real asset in your balance sheet.

AMANDA [*triumphant*] Aha! [*To Pliny*] You go home to bed and reflect on that, old man.

PROTEUS: Well, sir? Are you satisfied that we have the best paid proletariat in the world on our side?

MAGNUS [*gravely*] I dread revolution.

All except the two women laugh uproariously at this.

BOANERGES: I must join them there, sir. I am as much against chocolate creams as you are: they never agree with me. But a revolution in England!!! Put that out of your head, sir. Not if you were to tear up Magna Carta in Trafalgar Square, and light the fires of Smithfield to burn every member of the House of Commons.

MAGNUS: I was not thinking of a revolution in England. I was thinking of the countries on whose tribute we are living. Suppose it occurs to them to stop paying it! That has happened before.

PLINY: Oh no, sir: no, no, no. What would become of their foreign trade with us?

MAGNUS: At a pinch, I think they could do without the Christmas crackers.

CRASSUS: Oh, thats childish.

MAGNUS: Children in their innocence are sometimes very practical, Mr Colonial Secretary. The more I see of the sort of prosperity that comes of your leaving our vital industries to big business men as long as they keep your constituents quiet with high wages, the more I feel as if I were sitting on a volcano.

LYSISTRATA [*who has been listening with implacable contempt to the discussion, suddenly breaks in a sepulchral contralto*] Hear hear! My department was perfectly able and ready to deal with the supply of power from the tides in the north of Scotland, and you gave it away, like the boobs you are, to the Pentland Firth Syndicate: a gang of foreign capitalists who will make billions out of it at the people's expense while we are bungling and squabbling. Crassus worked that. His uncle is chairman.

CRASSUS: A lie. A flat lie. He is not related to me. He is only my stepson's father-in-law.

BALBUS: I demand an explanation of the words bungling and squabbling. We have had quite enough of them here today. Who are you getting at? It was not I who bungled the Factory Bill. I found it on my desk when I took office, with all His Majesty's suggestions in the margin; and you know it.

PROTEUS: Have you all done playing straight into His Majesty's hand, and making my situation here impossible? *Guilty silence.*

PROTEUS [*proceeding deliberately and authoritatively*] The question before us is not one of our manners and our abilities. His Majesty will not press that question, because if he did he would oblige us to raise the question of his own morals.

MAGNUS [*starts*] What!

BALBUS: Good, Joe!

CRASSUS [*aside to Amanda*] Thats got him.

MAGNUS: Am I to take that threat seriously, Mr. Proteus?

PROTEUS: If you try to prejudice what is a purely constitutional question by personal scandal, it will be easy enough for us to throw your mud back. In this conflict we are the challengers. You have the choice of weapons. If you choose scandal, we'll take you on at that. Personally I shall deplore it if you do. No good will come of washing our dirty linen in public. But dont make any mistake as to what will happen. I will be plain with you: I will dot the Is and cross the Ts. You will say that Crassus is a jobber.

CRASSUS [*springing up*] I—

PROTEUS [*fiercely crushing him*] Sit down. Leave this to me.

CRASSUS [*sits*] I a jobber! Well!

PROTEUS [*continuing*] You will say that I should never have given the Home Office to a bully like Balbus—

BALBUS [*intimidated by the fate of* Crassus, *but unable to forbear a protest*] Look here, Joe—

PROTEUS: You shut up, Bert. It's true.

BALBUS [*subsides with a shrug*]!

PROTEUS: Well, what will happen? There will be no denials, no excuses, no vindications. We shall not fall into that trap, clever as you are at setting it. Crassus will say just simply that you are a freethinker. And Balbus will say that you are a libertine.

THE MALE CABINET [*below their breaths*] Aha-a-a-a-h!!!

PROTEUS: Now, King Magnus! Our cards are on the table. What have you to say?

MAGNUS: Admirably put! People ask how it is that with all these strong characters around you hold your own as the only possible Prime Minister, in spite of your hysterics and tantrums, your secretiveness and your appalling laziness—

BALBUS [*delighted*] Hear hear! Youre getting it now, Joe.

MAGNUS [*continuing*] But when the decisive moment comes, they find out what a wonderful man you are.

PROTEUS: I am not a wonderful man. There is not a man or woman here whose job I could do as well as they do it. I am Prime Minister for the same reason that all Prime Ministers have been Prime Ministers: because I am good for nothing else. But I can keep to the point—when it suits me. And I can keep you to the point, sir, whether it suits you or not.

MAGNUS: At all events you do not flatter kings. One of them, at least, is grateful to you for that.

PROTEUS: Kings, as you and I very well know, rule their ministers by flattering them; and now that you are the only king left in the civilized half of Europe Nature seems to have concentrated in you all the genius for flattery that she used to have to divide between half a dozen kings, three emperors, and a Sultan.

MAGNUS: But what interest has a king in flattering a subject?

AMANDA: Suppose she's a goodlooking woman, sir!

NICOBAR: Suppose he has a lot of money, and the king's hard up!

PROTEUS: Suppose he is a Prime Minister, and you can do nothing except by his advice.

MAGNUS [*smiling with his utmost charm*] Ah, there you have hit the nail on the head. Well, I suppose I must surrender. I am beaten. You are all too clever for me.

BOANERGES: Well, nothing can be fairer than that.

PLINY [*rubbing his hands*] You are a gentleman, sir. We shant rub it in, you know.

BALBUS: Ever the best of friends. I am the last to kick a man when he's down.

CRASSUS: I may be a jobber; but nobody shall say that I am an ungenerous opponent.

BOANERGES [*suddenly overwhelmed with emotion, rises and begins singing in stentorian tones*]

Should auld acquaintance be forgot,
And never brought to mind—

Amanda bursts into uncontrollable laughter. The King looks reproachfully at her, struggling hard to keep his countenance. The others are beginning to join in the chorus when Proteus rises in a fury.

PROTEUS: Are you all drunk?

Dead silence. Boanerges sits down hastily. The other singers pretend that they have disapproved of his minstrelsy.

PROTEUS: You are at present engaged in a tug of war with the King: the tug of your lives. You think you have won. You havnt. All that has happened is that the King has let go the rope. You are sprawling on your backs; and he is laughing at you. Look at him! [*He sits down contemptuously*].

MAGNUS [*making no further attempt to conceal his merriment*] Come to my rescue, Amanda. It was you who set me off.

AMANDA [*wreathed with smiles*] You got me so nicely, sir. [*To Boanerges*] Bill: you are a great boob.

BOANERGES: I dont understand this. I understood His Majesty to give way to us in, I must say, the handsomest manner. Cant we take our victory like gentlemen?

MAGNUS: Perhaps I had better explain. I quite appreciate the frank and magnanimous spirit—may I say the English spirit?—in which my little concession has been received, especially by you, Mr Boanerges. But in truth it leaves matters just where they were; for I should never have dreamt of entering on a campaign of recrimination such as the Prime Minister suggested. As he has reminded you, my own character is far too vulnerable. A king is not allowed the luxury of a good character. Our country has produced millions of blameless green-grocers, but not one blameless monarch. I have to rule over more religious sects than I can count. To rule them impartially I must not belong to any of them; and they all regard people who do not belong to them as atheists. My court includes several perfectly respectable wives and mothers whose strange vanity it is to be talked about as abandoned females. To gain the reputation of being the king's mistress they would do almost anything except give the unfortunate monarch the pleasure of substantiating their claim. Side by side with them are the ladies who are really unscrupulous. They are so careful of their reputations that they lose no opportunity of indignantly denying that they have ever yielded to solicitations which have in fact never been made to them. Thus, every king is supposed to be a libertine; and as, oddly enough, he owes a great part of his popularity to this belief, he cannot deny it without deeply disappointing his subjects.

There is a rather grim silence, during which the King looks round in vain for some encouraging response.

LYSISTRATA [*severely*] Your Majesty's private affairs do not concern us, in any case.

AMANDA [*splutters into an irrepressible laugh*]!!!

MAGNUS [*looks reproachfully at Amanda*]!

AMANDA [*composing her features as best she can*] Excuse me.

CRASSUS: I hope your Majesty recognizes that kings are not the only people to whom certain sorts of mud always stick, no matter what fool throws them. Call a minister a jobber—

BALBUS: Or a bungler.

CRASSUS: Yes, or a bungler, and everybody believes it. Jobbery and incompetence are the two sorts of mud that stick to us, no matter how honest or capable we are; and we havnt the royal advantage that you enjoy, that the more the ladies take away your character the better the people like you.

BOANERGES [*suddenly*] Prime Minister: will you tell me what the Postmistress General is sniggering at?

AMANDA: This a free country, Bill. A sense of humor is not a crime. And when the King is not setting me off, you are.

BOANERGES: Where is the joke? I dont see it.

AMANDA: If you could see a joke, Bill, you wouldnt be the great popular orator you are.

BOANERGES: Thank Heaven, I am not a silly giggler like some I could mention.

AMANDA: Thanks, dearest Bill. Now, Joe: dont you think you have let us run loose long enough? What about that ultimatum?

MAGNUS [*shaking his head at her*] Traitor!

PROTEUS: I am in no hurry. His Majesty's speeches are very wise and interesting; and your back chat amuses both you and him. But the ultimatum is here all the time; and I shall not leave this room until I have His Majesty's signed pledge that its conditions will be observed.

All become gravely attentive.

MAGNUS: What are its terms?

PROTEUS: First, no more royal speeches.

MAGNUS: What! Not even if you dictate them?

PROTEUS: Not even if we dictate them. Your Majesty has a way of unrolling the manuscript and winking—

MAGNUS: Winking!

PROTEUS: You know what I mean. The best speech in the world can be read in such a way as to set the audience laughing at it. We have had enough of that. So, in future, no speeches.

MAGNUS: A dumb king?

PROTEUS: Of course we cannot object to such speeches as 'We declare this foundation stone well and truly laid' and so forth. But politically, yes: a dumb king.

PLINY [*to soften it*] A constitutional king.

PROTEUS [*implacably*] A dumb king.

MAGNUS: Hm! What next?

PROTEUS: The working of the Press from the palace back stairs must cease.

MAGNUS: You know that I have no control of the Press. The Press is in the hands of men much richer than I, who would not insert a single paragraph against their own interests even if it were signed by my own hand and sent to them with a royal command.

PROTEUS: We know that. But though these men are richer than you, they are not cleverer. They get amusing articles, spiced with exclusive backstairs information, that dont seem to them to have anything to do with politics. The next thing they know is that their pet shares have dropped fifteen points; that capital is frightened off their best prospectuses; and that some of the best measures in our party program are made to look like city jobs.

MAGNUS: Am I supposed to write these articles?

NICOBAR: Your man Sempronius does. I can spot his fist out of fifty columns.

CRASSUS: So can I. When he is getting at me he always begins the sentence with "Singularly enough."

PLINY [*chuckling*] Thats his trademark. "Singularly enough." Ha! ha!

MAGNUS: Is there to be any restriction on the other side? I have noticed, for instance, that in a certain newspaper which loses no opportunity of disparaging the throne, the last sentence of the leading article almost invariably begins with the words 'Once for all.' Whose trademark is that?

PROTEUS: Mine.

MAGNUS: Frank, Mr. Proteus.

PROTEUS: I know when to be frank. I learnt the trick from Your Majesty.

AMANDA [*tries not to laugh*]!

MAGNUS [*gently reproachful*] Amanda: what is the joke now? I am surprised at you.

AMANDA: Joe frank! When I want to find out what he is up to I have to come and ask your Majesty.

LYSISTRATA: That is perfectly true. In this Cabinet there is no such thing as a policy. Every man plays for his own hand.

NICOBAR: It's like a game of cards.

BALBUS: Only there are no partners.

LYSISTRATA: Except Crassus and Nicobar.

PLINY: Good, Lizzie! He! he! he!

NICOBAR: What do you mean?

LYSISTRATA: You know quite well what I mean. When will you learn, Nicobar, that it is no use trying to browbeat me. I began life as a schoolmistress; and I can browbeat any man in this Cabinet or out of it if he is fool enough to try to compete with me in that department.

BOANERGES: Order! order! Cannot the Prime Minister check these unseemly personalities?

PROTEUS: They give me time to think, Bill. When you have had as much parliamentary experience as I have you will be very glad of an interruption occasionally. May I proceed? *Silence.*

PROTEUS: His Majesty asks whether the restriction on press campaigning is to be entirely onesided. That, I take it, sir, is your question.

MAGNUS [*nods assent*]!

PROTEUS: The answer is in the affirmative.

BALBUS: Good!

MAGNUS: Anything more?

PROTEUS: Yes: one thing more. The veto must not be mentioned again. That can apply to both sides, if you like. The veto is dead.

MAGNUS: May we not make a historical reference to the corpse?

PROTEUS: No. I cannot carry on the King's government unless I can give pledges and carry them out. What is my pledge worth if our constituents are reminded every day that the King may veto anything that Parliament does? Do you expect me to say, when I am asked for a pledge, 'You must ask the King'?

MAGNUS: I have to say 'You must ask the Prime Minister.'

PLINY [*consoling him*] Thats the constitution, you know.

MAGNUS: Quite. I only mention it to shew that the Prime Minister does not really wish to kill the veto. He only wishes to move it next door.

PROTEUS: The people live next door. The name on the brass plate is Public Opinion.

MAGNUS [*gravely*] Admirably turned, Mr. Prime Minister; but unreal. I am far more subject to public opinion than you, because, thanks to the general belief in democracy, you can always pretend that what you do is done by the will of the people, who, God knows, never dreamt of it, and would not have understood it if they had; whereas, for what a king does, he, and he alone, is held responsible. A demagogue may steal a horse where a king dare not look over a hedge.

LYSISTRATA: I doubt if that is any longer true, sir. I know that I get blamed for everything that goes wrong in my department.

MAGNUS: Ah! But what a despot you are, Lysistrata! Granted, however, that the people have found out long ago that democracy is humbug, and that instead of establishing responsible government it has abolished it, do you not see what this means?

BOANERGES [*scandalized*] Steady, steady! I cannot sit here and listen to such a word as humbug being applied to democracy. I am sorry, sir; but with all respect for you, I really must draw the line at that.

MAGNUS: You are right, Mr. Boanerges, as you always are. Democracy is a very real thing, with much less humbug about it than many older institutions. But it means, not that the people govern, but that the responsibility and the veto now belong neither to kings nor demagogues as such, but to whoever is clever enough to get them.

LYSISTRATA: Yourself, sir, for example?

MAGNUS: I think I am in the running. That is why I do not feel bound to accept this ultimatum. By signing it I put myself out of the running. Why should I?

BALBUS: Because youre the king: thats why.

MAGNUS: Does it follow?

PROTEUS: If two men ride the same horse, one must ride behind.

LYSISTRATA: Which?

PROTEUS [*turning to her sharply*] What was that you said?

LYSISTRATA [*with placid but formidable obstinacy and ironical explicitness*] I said Which? You said that if two men rode the same horse one of them must ride behind. I said Which? [*Explanatorily*] Which man must ride behind?

AMANDA: Got it, Joe?

PROTEUS: That is exactly the question that has to be settled here and now.

AMANDA: 'Once for all.'

Everybody laughs except Proteus, who rises in a fury.

PROTEUS: I will not stand this perpetual tomfooling. I had rather be a dog than the Prime Minister of a country where the only things the inhabitants can be serious about are football and refreshments. Lick the King's boots: that is all you are fit for. [*He dashes out of the room*].

BALBUS: Youve done it now, Mandy. I hope youre proud of yourself.

MAGNUS: It is you, Amanda, who should go and coax him back. But I suppose I must do it myself, as usual. Excuse me, ladies and gentlemen.

He rises. The rest rise. He goes out.

BOANERGES: I told you. I told you what would come of conducting a conference with His Majesty as if it were a smoking concert. I am disgusted. [*He flings himself back into his chair*].

BALBUS: We'd just cornered the old fox; and then Amanda must have her silly laugh and lets him out of it [*he sits*].

NICOBAR: What are we to do now? thats what I want to know.

AMANDA [*incorrigible*] I suggest a little community singing [*she makes conductorlike gestures*].

NICOBAR: Yah!! [*he sits down very sulkily*].

AMANDA [*sits down with a little splutter of laughter*]!

CRASSUS [*thoughtful*] Take it easy, friends. Joe knows what he is about.

LYSISTRATA: Of course he does. I can excuse you, Bill, because it's your first day in the Cabinet. But if the rest of you havnt found out by this time that Joe's rages are invariably calculated, then nothing will ever teach you anything [*she sits down contemptuously*].

BOANERGES [*in his grandest manner*] Well, Madam, I know I am a newcomer: everything must have a beginning. I am open to argument and conviction. The Prime Minister brought this conference, in what I admit was a very able and resolute manner, to the verge of a decision. Then, in a fit of childish temper he breaks up the conference, leaving us looking like fools with nothing done. And you tell me he did it on purpose! Where was the advantage to him in such a display? answer me that.

LYSISTRATA: He is settling the whole business with the King behind our backs. That is what Joe always contrives to do, by hook or crook.

PLINY: You didnt arrange it with him, Mandy: did you?

AMANDA: There wasnt any need to arrange it. Joe can always depend on one or other of us saying something that will give him an excuse for flying out.

CRASSUS: In my opinion, ladies and gentlemen, we have done our bit, and may leave the rest to Joe. Matters had reached a point at which it was yes or no between the Cabinet and the Crown. There is only one sort of committee that is better than a committee of two; and that is a committee of one. Like the family in Wordsworth's poem, we are seven—

LYSISTRATA: Eight.

CRASSUS: Well, seven or eight, we were too many for the final grapple. Two persons sticking to the point are worth eight all over the shop. So my advice is that we just sit here quietly until Joe comes back and tells us whats been settled. Perhaps Amanda will oblige with a song. [*He resumes his seat*].

The King returns with Proteus, who looks glum. All rise. The two resume their seats in silence. The rest sit down.

MAGNUS [*very grave*] The Prime Minister has been good enough to pursue the discussion with me in private to a point at which the issue is now clear. If I do not accept the ultimatum I shall receive your resignations and his; and the country will learn from his explanatory speech in the House of Commons that it is to choose between Cabinet government and monarchical government: an issue on which I frankly say that I should be very sorry to win, as I cannot carry on without the support of a body of ministers whose existence gives the English people a sensation of self-government.

AMANDA [*splutters*]!

CRASSUS [*whispers*] Shut up, will you?

MAGNUS [*continuing*] Naturally I want to avert a conflict in which success would damage me and failure disable me. But you tell me that I can do so only by signing pledges which would make me a mere Lord Chamberlain, without even the despotism which he exercises over the theatre. I should sink below the level of the meanest of my subjects, my sole privilege being that of being shot at when some victim of misgovernment resorts to assassination to avenge himself. How am I to defend myself? You are many: I oppose you single-handed. There was a time when the king could depend on the support of the aristocracy and the cultivated bourgeoisie. Today there is not a single aristocrat left in politics, not a single member of the professions, not a single leading personage in big business or finance. They are richer than ever, more powerful than ever, more able and better educated than ever. But not one of them will touch this drudgery of government, this public work that never ends because we cannot finish one job without creating ten fresh ones. We get no thanks for it because ninety-nine hundredths of it is unknown to the people, and the remaining hundredth is resented by them as an invasion of their liberty or an increase in their taxation. It wears out the strongest man, and even the strongest woman, in five or six years. It slows down to nothing when we are fresh from our holidays and best able to bear it, and rises in an overwhelming wave through some unforeseen catastrophe when we are on the verge of nervous breakdown from overwork and fit for rest and sleep only. And this drudgery, remember, is a sweated trade, the only one now left in this country. My civil list leaves me a poor man among multi-millionaires. Your salaries can be earned ten times over in the city by anyone with outstanding organizing or administrative ability. History tells us that the first Lord Chancellor who abandoned the woolsack for the city boardroom struck the nation with amazement: today the nation would be equally amazed if a man of his ability thought it worth his while to prefer the woolsack even to the stool of an office boy as a jumping-off place for his ambition. Our work is no longer even respected. It is looked down on by our men of genius as dirty work. What great actor would exchange his stage? what great barrister his court? what great preacher his pulpit? for the squalor of the political arena in which we have to struggle with foolish factions in parliament and with ignorant voters in the constituencies? The scientists will have nothing to do with us; for the atmosphere of politics is not the atmosphere of science. Even political science, the science by which civilization must live or die, is busy explaining the past whilst we have to grapple with the present: it leaves the ground before our feet in black darkness whilst it lights up every corner of the landscape behind us. All the talent and genius of the country is bought up by the flood of unearned money. On that poisoned wealth talent and genius live far more luxuriously in the service of the rich than we in the service of our country. Politics, once the centre of attraction for ability, public spirit, and ambition, has now become the refuge of a few fanciers of public speaking and party intrigue who find all the other avenues to distinction closed to them either by their lack of practical ability, their comparative poverty and lack of education, or, let me hasten to add, their hatred of oppression and injustice, and their contempt for the chicaneries and false pretences of commercialized professionalism. History tells us of a gentleman-statesman who declared that such people were not fit to govern. Within a year it was discovered that they could govern at least as well as anyone else who could be persuaded to take on the job. Then began that abandonment of politics by the old governing class which has ended in all Cabinets, conservative no less than progressive, being what were called in the days of that rash statesman Labor Cabinets. Do not misunderstand me: I do not want the old governing class back. It governed so selfishly that the people would have perished if democracy had not swept it out of politics. But evil as it was in many ways, at least it stood above the tyranny of popular ignorance and popular poverty. Today only the king stands above that tyranny. You are dangerously subject to it. In spite of my urgings and remonstrances you have not yet dared to take command of our schools and put a stop to the inculcation upon your unfortunate children of superstitions and prejudices that stand like stone walls across every forward path. Are you well advised in trying to reduce me to your own slavery to them? If I do not stand above them there is no longer any reason for my existence at all. I stand for the future and the past, for the posterity that has no vote and the tradition that never had any. I stand for the great abstractions: for conscience and virtue; for the eternal against the expedient; for the evolutionary appetite against the day's guttony; for intellectual integrity, for humanity, for the rescue of industry from commercialism and of science from professionalism, for everything that you desire as sincerely as I, but which in you is held in leash by the Press, which can organize against you the ignorance and superstition, the timidity and credulity, the gullibility and prudery, the hating and hunting instinct of the voting mob, and cast you down from power if you utter a word to alarm or displease the adventurers who have the Press in their pockets. Between you and that tyranny stands the throne. I have no elections to fear; and if any newspaper magnate dares offend me, that magnate's fashionable wife and marriageable daughters will soon make him understand that the King's displeasure is still a sentence of social death within range of St. James's Palace. Think of the things you dare not do! the persons you dare not offend! Well, a king with a little courage may tackle them for you. Responsibilities which would break your backs may still be borne on a king's shoulders. But he must be a king, not a puppet. You would be responsible for a puppet: remember that. But whilst you continue to support me as a separate and independent estate of the realm, I am your scapegoat: you get the credit of all our popular legislation whilst you put the odium of all our resistance to ignorant popular clamor on me. I ask you, before you play your last card and destroy me, to consider where you will be without me. Think once: think twice: for your danger is, not that

I may defeat you, but that your success is certain if you insist.

LYSISTRATA: Splendid!

AMANDA: You did speak that piece beautifully, sir.

BALBUS [*grumbling*] All very well; but what about my brother-in-law Mike?

LYSISTRATA [*maddened*] Oh, confound your brother-in-law Mike!

BOANERGES: Order! order!

LYSISTRATA [*to the King*] I beg your pardon, sir; but really—at a moment like this—[*words fail her*].

MAGNUS [*to Balbus*] If I had not put my foot down, Mr Balbus, the Prime Minister would have been unable to keep your brother-in-law out of the Cabinet.

BALBUS [*aggressively*] And why should he not be in the Cabinet?

AMANDA: Booze, my Balby: booze. Raising the elbow!

BALBUS [*bullying*] Who says so?

AMANDA: I do, darling.

BALBUS [*subsiding*] Well, perhaps it would surprise you all to know that Mike doesnt drink as much as I do.

AMANDA: You carry it better, Bert.

PLINY: Mike never knows when to stop.

CRASSUS: The time for Mike to stop is before he begins, if you ask me.

LYSISTRATA [*impetuously*] What sort of animals are you—you men? The King puts before us the most serious question of principle we shall ever have to deal with; and off you start discussing whether this drunken wretch takes honest whisky like Balbus or methylated spirit or petrol or whatever he can lay his hands on when the fit takes him.

BALBUS: I agree with that. What does it matter what Mike drinks? What does it matter whether he drinks or not? Mike would strengthen the Cabinet because he represents Breakages, Limited, the biggest industrial corporation in the country.

LYSISTRATA [*letting herself go*] Just so! Breakages, Limited! just so! Listen to me, sir; and judge whether I have not reason to feel everything you have just said to the very marrow of my bones. Here am I, the Powermistress Royal. I have to organize and administer all the motor power in the country for the good of the country. I have to harness the winds and the tides, the oils and the coal seams. I have to see that every little sewing machine in the Hebrides, every dentist's drill in Shetland, every carpet sweeper in Margate, has its stream of driving power on tap from a switch in the wall as punctually as the great thundering dynamos of our big industrial plants. I do it; but it costs twice as much as it should. Why? Because every new invention is bought up and suppressed by Breakages, Limited. Every breakdown, every accident, every smash and crash, is a job for them. But for them we should have unbreakable glass, unbreakable steel, imperishable materials of all sorts. But for them our goods trains could be started and stopped without battering and tearing the vitals out of every wagon and sending it to their repair shops once a week instead of once a year. Our national repair bill runs up to hundreds of millions. I could name you a dozen inventions within my own term of office which would have effected enormous economies in breakages and breakdowns; but these people can afford to pay an inventor more for his machine or his process or whatever it may be than he could hope to make by a legitimate use of it; and when they have bought it they smother it. When the inventor is poor and not good at defending himself they make bogus trials of his machine and report that it is no use. I have been shot at twice by inventors driven crazy by this sort of thing: they blamed me for it—as if I could stand up against this monster with its millions and its newspapers and its fingers in every pie. It is heartbreaking. I love my department: I dream of nothing but its efficiency: with me it comes before every personal tie, every happiness that common women run after. I would give my right hand to see these people in the bankruptcy court with half their business abolished and the other half done in public workshops where public losses are not private gains. You stand for that, sir; and I would be with you to the last drop of my blood if I dared. But what can I do? If I said one word of this in public, not a week would pass in the next two years without an article on the inefficiency and corruption of all Government departments, especially departments managed, like mine, by females. They would dig up the very machines they have buried, and make out that it is my fault that they have never been brought into use. They would set their private police to watch me day and night to get something against my private character. One of their directors told me to my face that by lifting up his finger he could get my windows broken by the mob; and that Breakages, Limited, would get the job of putting in new glass. And it is true. It is infamous; it is outrageous; but if I attempt to fight them I shall be hounded out of public life, and they will shove Mouldly Mike into the Cabinet to run my department in their interests: that is, to make such a failure of it that Joe will have to sell it to Breakages, Limited, at scrap iron prices. I—I—oh, it is beyond bearing [*she breaks down*].

There is a troubled silence for a moment. Then the voice of the Prime Minister breaks it impressively as he addresses the King.

PROTEUS: You hear that, sir. Your one supporter in the Cabinet admits that the industrial situation is too strong for her. I do not pretend to be able to control the women in my Cabinet; but not one of them dare support you.

AMANDA [*springing up*] Whats that? Not dare! What do you bet that I dont go down to Mouldy Mike's constituency and say everything that Lizzie has said and a lot more too, if I choose? I tell you, Breakages, Limited, never interferes in my department. I'd like to catch them at it.

MAGNUS: I am afraid that that is only because the efficiency of the Post Office is as important to them as to the general public.

AMANDA: Stuff! They could get rid of me without shutting up the Post Office. Theyre afraid of me—of me, Amanda Postlethwaite.

MAGNUS: You coax them, I am afraid.

AMANDA: Coax! What do you think they care for coaxing? They can have all the coaxing they want from younger and prettier women than I by paying for it. No use trying to coax that lot. Intimidate them: thats the way to handle them.

LYSISTRATA [*her voice still broken*] I wish I could intimidate them.

MAGNUS: But what can Amanda do that you cannot do?

AMANDA: I'll tell you. She cant mimic people. And she cant sing funny songs. I can do both; and that—with all respect, sir—makes me the real queen of England.

BOANERGES: Oh, come! Disgraceful! Shame!

AMANDA: If you provoke me, Bill, I'll drive you out of your constituency inside of two months.

BOANERGES: Ho! You will, will you? How?

AMANDA: Just as I drove the Chairman of Breakages out of my own constituency when he came down there and tried to take my seat from me.

MAGNUS: I never quite understood why he turned tail. How did you do it?

AMANDA: I'll tell you. He opened his campaign with a great Saturday night speech against me in the Home Lovers' Hall to five thousand people. In that same hall a week later, I faced a meeting of the very same people. I didnt argue. I mimicked him. I took all the high-falutin passages in his speech, and repeated them in his best manner until I had the whole five thousand laughing at him. Then I asked them would they like me to sing; and their Yes nearly lifted the roof off. I had two songs. They both had choruses. One went 'She lets me go out on Saturday night, on Saturday night, on Saturday night'— like that. The other went "Boo! Hoo! I want Amanda's Teddy bear to play with." They sang it under the windows of his hotel next time he came. He cancelled his meeting and left. And thats how England is governed by yours truly, sir. Lucky for England that Queen Amanda is a good sort, in spite of some surface faults. [*She resumes her seat with triumphant self-satisfaction*].

BALBUS: Lucky for England theres only one of you: thats what *I* say.

AMANDA [*wafts him a kiss*]!

MAGNUS: Should not The Queen support the King, your Majesty?

AMANDA: Sorry, sir; but there isnt room for two monarchs in my realm. I am against you on principle because the talent for mimicry isnt hereditary.

PROTEUS: Now, anybody else? We have heard why the two ladies cannot support the King. Is there anybody who can? *Silence.*

MAGNUS: I see that my appeal has been in vain. I do not reproach you, ladies and gentlemen, because I perceive that your situation is a difficult one. The question is, how to change it.

NICOBAR: Sign the ultimatum: that is how.

MAGNUS: I am not quite convinced of that. The Home Secretary's brother-in-law was quite willing to sign the pledge of total abstinence if I would admit him to the Cabinet. His offer was not accepted, because, though none of us doubted that he would sign the pledge, we were not equally certain that the infirmities of his nature would allow him to keep it. My nature is also subject to infirmity. Are you satisfied, Mr. Proteus, that if I sign this ultimatum, I shall not inevitably relapse into the conduct that my nature dictates?

PROTEUS [*his patience strained*] What is the use of going on like this? You are a man on the scaffold, spinning out his prayers to put off the inevitable execution as long as possible. Nothing that you can say will make any difference. You know you must sign. Why not sign and have done with it?

NICOBAR: Now youre talking, Joe.

BALBUS: Thats the stuff to give him.

PLINY: Gulp it down, sir. It wont get any sweeter by keeping: what?

LYSISTRATA: Oh, for God's sake, sign, sir. This is torture to me.

MAGNUS: I perceive, gentlemen, that I have come to the end of your patience. I will tax it no further: you have been very forbearing; and I thank you for it. I will say no more by way of discussion; but I must have until five o'clock this evening to consider my decision. At that hour, if I can find no other way out, I will sign without another word. Meanwhile, ladies and gentlemen, au revoir!

He rises. All rise. He marches out.

PROTEUS: His last wriggle. Never mind: we have him safe enough. What about lunch? I am starving. Will you have lunch with me, Lizzie.

LYSISTRATA: Dont speak to me. [*She rushes out distractedly*].

AMANDA: Poor darling Lizzie! She's a regular old true blue Diehard. If only I had her brains and education! or if she had my variety talent! what a queen she'd make! Like old Queen Elizabeth, eh? Dont grieve, Joe: I'll lunch with you since youre so pressing.

CRASSUS: Come and lunch with me—all of you.

AMANDA: What opulence! Can you afford it?

CRASSUS: Breakages will pay. They have a standing account at the Ritz. Over five thousand a year, it comes to.

PROTEUS: Right. Let us spoil the Egyptians.

BOANERGES [*with Roman dignity*] My lunch will cost me one and sixpence; and I shall pay for it myself [*he stalks out*].

AMANDA [*calling after him*] Dont make a beast of yourself, Bill. Ta ta!

PROTEUS: Come on, come on: it's ever so late.

They all hurry out. Sempronius and Pamphilius, entering, have to stand aside to let them pass before returning to their desks. Proteus, with Amanda on his arm, stops in the doorway on seeing them.

PROTEUS: Have you two been listening, may I ask?

PAMPHILIUS: Well, it would be rather inconvenient wouldnt it, if we had to be told everything that passed?

SEMPRONIUS: Once for all, Mr. Proteus, the King's private secretaries must hear everything, see everything, and know everything.

PROTEUS: Singularly enough, Mr. Sempronius, I havnt the slightest objection [*he goes*].

AMANDA [*going with him*] Goodbye, Semmy. So long, Pam.

PAMPHILIUS } [*seating themselves at their writing tables*
SEMPRONIUS } *and yawning prodigiously*] Ou-ou-ou-ou-ou-fff!!!

AN INTERLUDE

Orinthia's boudoir at half-past fifteen on the same day. She is at her writing-table scribbling notes. She is romantically beautiful, and beautifully dressed. As the table is against the wall near a corner, with the other wall on her left, her back alone is visible from the middle of the room. The door is near the corner diagonally opposite. There is a large settee in the middle of the room.

The King enters and waits on the threshold.

ORINTHIA [*crossly, without looking round*] Who is that?

MAGNUS: His Majesty the King.

ORINTHIA: I dont want to see him.

MAGNUS: How soon will you be disengaged?

ORINTHIA: I didnt say I was engaged. Tell the king I dont want to see him.

MAGNUS: He awaits your pleasure [*he comes in and seats himself on the settee*].

ORINTHIA: Go away. [*A pause*]. I wont speak to you. [*Another pause*]. If my private rooms are to be broken into at any moment because they are in the palace, and the king is not a gentleman, I must take a house outside. I am writing to the agents about one now.

MAGNUS: What is our quarrel today, belovéd?

ORINTHIA: Ask your conscience.

MAGNUS: I have none when you are concerned. You must tell me.

She takes a book from the table and rises; then sweeps superbly forward to the settee and flings the book into his hands.

ORINTHIA: There!

MAGNUS: What is this?

ORINTHIA: Page 16. Look at it.

MAGNUS [*looking at the title on the back of the book*] 'Songs of our Great Great Grandparents.' What page did you say?

ORINTHIA [*between her teeth*] Six-teen.

MAGNUS [*opening the book and finding the page, his eye lighting up with recognition as he looks at it*] Ah! The Pilgrim of Love!

ORINTHIA: Read the first three words—if you dare.

MAGNUS [*smiling as he caresses the phrase*] 'Orinthia, my belovéd'.

ORINTHIA: The name you pretended to invent specially for me, the only women in the world for you. Picked up out of the rubbish basket in a secondhand bookseller's! And I thought you were a poet!

MAGNUS: Well, one poet may consecrate a name for another. Orinthia is a name full of magic for me. It could not be that if I had invented it myself. I heard it at a concert of ancient music when I was a child; and I have treasured it ever since.

ORINTHIA: You always have a pretty excuse. You are the King of liars and humbugs. You cannot understand how a falsehood like that wounds me.

MAGNUS [*remorsefully, stretching out his arms towards her*] Beloved: I am sorry.

ORINTHIA: Put your hands in your pockets: they shall not touch me ever again.

MAGNUS [*obeying*] Dont pretend to be hurt unless you really are, dearest. It wrings my heart.

ORINTHIA: Since when have you set up a heart? Did you buy that, too, secondhand?

MAGNUS: I have something in me that winces when you are hurt—or pretend to be.

ORINTHIA [*contemptuously*] Yes: I have only to squeal, and you will take me up and pet me as you would a puppy run over by a car. [*Sitting down beside him, but beyond arm's length*] That is what you give me when my heart demands love. I had rather you kicked me.

MAGNUS: I should like to kick you sometimes, when you are specially aggravating. But I shouldnt do it well. I should be afraid of hurting you all the time.

ORINTHIA: I believe you would sign my death warrant without turning a hair.

MAGNUS: That is true, in a way. It is wonderful how subtle your mind is, as far as it goes.

ORINTHIA: It does not go as far as yours, I suppose.

MAGNUS: I dont know. Our minds go together half way. Whether it is that your mind stops there or else that the road forks, and you take the high road and I take the low road, I cannot say; but somehow after a certain point we lose one another.

ORINTHIA: And then you go back to your Amandas and Lysistratas: creatures whose idea of romance is a minister in love with a department, and whose bedside books are blue books.

MAGNUS: They are not always thinking of some man or other. That is a rather desirable extension of their interests, in my opinion. If Lysistrata had a lover I should not be interested in him in the least; and she would bore me to distraction if she could talk of nothing else. But I am very much interested in her department. Her devotion to it gives us a topic of endless interest.

ORINTHIA: Well, go to her: I am not detaining you. But dont tell her that I have nothing to talk about but men; for that is a lie; and you know it.

MAGNUS: It is, as you say, a lie; and I know it. But I did not say it.

ORINTHIA: You implied it. You meant it. When those ridiculous political women are with us you talk to them all the time, and never say a word to me.

MAGNUS: Nor you to me. We cannot talk to one another in public: we have nothing to say that could be said before other people. Yet we find enough to say to one another when we are alone together. Would you change that if you could?

ORINTHIA: You are as slippery as an eel; but you shall not slip through my fingers. Why do you surround yourself with political bores and frumps and dowdy busybodies who cant talk: they can only debate about their dull departments and their fads and their election chances. [*Rising impatiently*] Who could talk to such people? If it were not for the nonentities of wives and husbands they drag about with them, there would be nobody to talk to at all. And even they can talk of nothing but the servants and the baby. [*Suddenly returning to her seat*] Listen to me, Mte. Why can you not be a real king?

Magnus: In what way, belovédest?

ORINTHIA: Send all these stupid people packing. Make them do their drudgeries in their departments without bothering you about it, as you make your servants here sweep the floors and dust the furniture. Live a really noble and beautiful life—a kingly life—with me. What you need to make you a real king is a real queen.

MAGNUS: But I have got one.

ORINTHIA: Oh, you are blind. You are worse than blind: you have low tastes. Heaven is offering you a rose; and you cling to a cabbage.

MAGNUS [*laughing*] That is a very apt metaphor, belovéd. But what wise man, if you force him to choose between doing without roses and doing without cabbages, would not secure the cabbages? Besides, all these old married cabbages were once roses; and, though young things like you dont remember that, their husbands do. They dont notice the change. Besides, you should know better than anyone else that when a man gets tired of his wife and leaves her it is never because she has lost her good looks. The new love is often older and uglier than the old.

ORINTHIA: Why should I know it better than anyone else?

MAGNUS: Why because you have been married twice; and both your husbands have run away from you to much plainer and stupider women. When I begged your present husband to come back to court for a while for the sake of appearances he said no man could call his soul his own in the same house with you. And yet that man was utterly infatuated with your beauty when he married you. Your first husband actually forced a good wife to divorce him so that he might marry you; but before two years were out he went back to her and died in her arms, poor chap.

ORINTHIA: Shall I tell you why these men could not live with me? It was because I am a thoroughbred, and they are only hacks. They had nothing against me: I was perfectly faithful to them. I kept their houses beautifully: I fed them better than they had ever been fed in their lives.

But because I was higher than they were, and greater, they could not stand the strain of trying to live up to me. So I let them go their way, poor wretches, back to their cabbages. Look at the old creature Ignatius is living with now! She gives you his real measure.

MAGNUS: An excellent woman. Ignatius is quite happy with her. I never saw a man so changed.

ORINTHIA: Just what he is fit for. Commonplace. Bourgeoise. She trots through the streets shopping. [*Rising*] I tread the plains of Heaven. Common women cannot come where I am; and common men find themselves out and slink away.

MAGNUS: It must be magnificent to have the consciousness of a goddess without ever doing a thing to justify it.

ORINTHIA: Give me a goddess's work to do; and I will do it. I will even stoop to a queen's work if you will share the throne with me. But do not pretend that people become great by doing great things. They do great things because they are great, if the great things come along. But they are great just the same when the great things do not come along. If I never did anything but sit in this room and powder my face and tell you what a clever fool you are, I should still be heavens high above the millions of common women who do their domestic duty, and sacrifice themselves, and run Trade departments and all the rest of the vulgarities. Has all the tedious public work you have done made you any the better? I have seen you before and after your boasted strokes of policy; and you were the same man, and would have been the same man to me and to yourself if you had never done them. Thank God my self-consciousness is something nobler than vulgar conceit in having done something. It is what I am, not what I do, that you must worship in me. If you want deeds, go to your men and women of action, as you call them, who are all in a conspiracy to pretend that the mechanical things they do, the foolhardy way they risk their worthless lives, or their getting up in the morning at four and working sixteen hours a day for thirty years, like coral insects, make them great. What are they for? these dull slaves? To keep the streets swept for me. To enable me to reign over them in beauty like the stars without having anything to do with their slavery except to console it, to dazzle it, to enable them to forget it in adoring dreams of me. Am I not worth it? [*She sits, fascinating him*]. Look into my eyes and tell the truth. Am I worth it or not?

MAGNUS: To me, who love beauty, yes. But you should hear the speeches Balbus makes about your pension.

ORINTHIA: And my debts: do not forget my debts, my mortgages, the bill of sale on my furniture, the thousands I have had from the moneylenders to save me from being sold up because I will not borrow from my friends. Lecture me again about them; but do not dare pretend that the people grudge me my pension. They glory in it, and in my extravagance, as you call it.

MAGNUS [*more gravely*] By the way, Orinthia, when your dressmakers took up that last bill for you, they were speculating, were they not, in your chances of becoming my queen some day?

ORINTHIA: Well, what if they were?

MAGNUS: They would hardly have ventured on that without a hint from somebody. Was it from you?

ORINTHIA: You think me capable of that! You have a very low side to you, Magnus.

MAGNUS: No doubt: like other mortal fabrics I have a wrong side and a right side. But it is no use your giving yourself airs, belovédest. You are capable of anything. Do you deny that there was some suggestion of the kind?

ORINTHIA: How dare you challenge me to deny it? I never deny. Of course there was a suggestion of the kind.

MAGNUS: I thought so.

ORINTHIA: Oh, stupid! stupid! Go keep a grocer's shop: that is what you are fit for. Do you suppose that the suggestion came from me? Why, you great oaf, it is in the air: when my dressmaker hinted at it I told her that if she ever dared to repeat such a thing she should never get another order from me. But can I help people seeing what is as plain as the sun in the heavens? [*Rising again*] Everyone knows that I am the real queen. Everyone treats me as the real queen. They cheer me in the streets. When I open one of the art exhibitions or launch a new ship they crowd the place out. I am one of Nature's queens; and they know it. If you do not, you are not one of Nature's kings.

MAGNUS: Sublime! Nothing but genuine inspiration could give a woman such cheek.

ORINTHIA: Yes: inspiration, not cheek. [*Sitting as before*] Magnus: When are you going to face my destiny, and your own?

MAGNUS: But my wife? The Queen? What is to become of my poor dear Jemima?

ORINTHIA: Oh, drown her: shoot her: tell your chauffeur to drive her into the Serpentine and leave her there. The woman makes you ridiculous.

MAGNUS: I dont think I should like that. And the public would think it illnatured.

ORINTHIA: Oh, you know what I mean. Divorce her. Make her divorce you. It is quite easy. That was how Ronny married me. Everybody does it when they need a change.

MAGNUS: But I cant imagine what I should do without Jemima.

ORINTHIA: Nobody else can imagine what you do with her. But you need not do without her. You can see as much of her as you like when we are married. I shall not be jealous and make scenes.

MAGNUS: That is very magnanimous of you. But I am afraid it does not settle the difficulty. Jemima would not think it right to keep up her present intimacy with me if I were married to you.

ORINTHIA: What a woman! Would she be in any worse position then than I am in now?

MAGNUS: No.

ORINTHIA: You mean, then, that you do not mind placing me in a position that you do not think good enough for her?

MAGNUS: Orinthia. I did not place you in your present position. You placed yourself in it. I could not resist you. You gathered me like a daisy.

ORINTHIA: Did you want to resist me?

MAGNUS: Oh no. I never resist temptation, because I have found that things that are bad for me do not tempt me.

ORINTHIA: Well, then, what are we talking about?

MAGNUS: I forget. I think I was explaining the impossibility of my wife changing places with you.

ORINTHIA: Why impossible, pray?

MAGNUS: I cannot make you understand: you see you have never been really married, though you have led two captives to the altar, and borne children to one of them. Being your husband is only a job for which one man will do as well as another, and which the last man holds subject to six months notice in the divorce court. Being my wife is something quite different. The smallest derogation to Jemima's dignity would hit me like the lash of a whip across the face. About yours, somehow, I do not care a rap.

ORINTHIA: Nothing can derogate from my dignity: it is divine. Hers is only a convention: that is why you tremble when it is challenged.

MAGNUS: Not a bit. It is because she is a part of my real workaday self. You belong to fairyland.

ORINTHIA: Suppose she dies! Will you die too?

MAGNUS: Not immediately. I shall have to carry on as best I can without her, though the prospect terrifies me.

ORINTHIA: Might not carrying on without her include marrying me?

MAGNUS: My dear Orinthia, I had rather marry the devil. Being a wife is not your job.

ORINTHIA: You think so because you have no imagination. And you dont know me because I have never let you really possess me. I should make you more happy than any man has ever yet been on earth.

MAGNUS: I defy you to make me more happy than our strangely innocent relations have already made me.

ORINTHIA [*rising restlessly*] You talk like a child or a saint. [*Turning on him*] I can give you a new life: one of which you have no conception. I can give you beautiful, wonderful children: have you ever seen a lovelier boy than my Basil?

MAGNUS: Your children are beautiful; but they are fairy children; and I have several very real ones already. A divorce would not sweep them out of the way of the fairies.

ORINTHIA: In short, when your golden moment comes—when the gates of heaven open before you, you are afraid to come out of your pigsty.

MAGNUS: If I am a pig, a pigsty is the proper place for me.

ORINTHIA: I cannot understand it. All men are fools and moral cowards when you come to know them. But you are less of a fool and less of a moral coward than any man I have ever known. You have almost the makings of a first rate woman in you. When I leave the earth and soar up to the regions which are my real eternal home, you can follow me: I can speak to you as I can speak to no one else; and you can say things to me that would just make your stupid wife cry. There is more of you in me than of any other man within my reach. There is more of me in you than of any other woman within your reach. We are meant for one another: it is written across the sky that you and I are queen and king. How can you hesitate? What attraction is there for you in your common healthy jolly lumps of children and your common housekeeper wife and the rabble of dowdies and upstarts and intriguers and clowns that think they are governing the country when they are only squabbling with you? Look again at me, man: again and again. Am I not worth a million such? Is not life with me as high above them as the sun is above the gutter?

MAGNUS: Yes yes yes yes, of course. You are lovely: you are divine [*she cannot restrain a gesture of triumph*]. And you are enormously amusing.

This anti-climax is too much for Orinthia's exaltation; but she is too clever not to appreciate it. With another gesture, this time of deflation, she sits down at his left hand with an air of suffering patience, and listens in silence to the harangue which follows.

MAGNUS: Some day perhaps Nature will graft the roses on the cabbages and make every woman as enchanting as you; and then what a glorious lark life will be! But at present, what I come here for is to enjoy talking to you like this when I need an hour's respite from royalty: when my stupid wife has been worrying me, or my jolly lumps of children bothering me, or my turbulent Cabinet obstructing me: when, as the doctors say, what I need is a change. You see, my dear, there is no wife on earth so precious, no children so jolly, no Cabinet so tactful that it is impossible ever to get tired of them. Jemima has her limitations, as you have observed. And I have mine. Now if our limitations exactly corresponded I should never want to talk to anyone else; and neither would she. But as that never happens, we are like all other married couples: that is, there are subjects which can never be discussed between us because they are sore subjects. There are people we avoid mentioning to one another because one of us likes them and the other doesnt. Not only individuals, but whole sorts of people. For instance, your sort. My wife doesnt like your sort, doesnt understand it, mistrusts and dreads it. Not without reason; for women like you are dangerous to wives. But I dont dislike your sort: I understand it, being a little in that line myself. At all events I am not afraid of it; though the least allusion to it brings a cloud over my wife's face. So when I want to talk freely about it I come and talk to you. And I take it she talks to friends of hers about people of whom she never talks to me. She has men friends from whom she can get some things that she cannot get from me. If she didnt do so she would be limited by my limitations, which would end in her hating me. So I always do my best to make her men friends feel at home with us.

ORINTHIA: A model husband in a model household! And when the model household becomes a bore, I am the diversion.

MAGNUS: Well, what more can you ask? Do not let us fall into the common mistake of expecting to become one flesh and one spirit. Every star has its own orbit; and between it and its nearest neighbor there is not only a powerful attraction but an infinite distance. When the attraction becomes stronger than the distance the two do not embrace: they crash together in ruin. We two also have our orbits, and must keep an infinite distance between us to avoid a disastrous collision. Keeping our distance is the whole secret of good manners; and without good manners human society is intolerable and impossible.

ORINTHIA: Would any other woman stand your sermons, and even like them?

MAGNUS: Orinthia: we are only two children at play; and you must be content to be my queen in fairyland. And [*rising*] I must go back to my work.

ORINTHIA: What work have you that is more important than being with me?

MAGNUS: None.

ORINTHIA: Then sit down.

MAGNUS: Unfortunately, this silly business of government must be carried on. And there is a crisis this evening, as usual.

ORINTHIA: But the crisis is not until five: I heard all about it from Sempronius: Why do you encourage that greedy schemer Proteus? He humbugs you. He humbugs everybody. He even humbugs himself; and of course he humbugs that Cabinet which is a disgrace to you: it is like an overcrowded third class carriage. Why do you allow such riffraff to waste your time? After all, what are you paid for? To be a king: that is, to wipe your boots on common people.

MAGNUS: Yes: but this king business, as the Americans call it, has got itself so mixed up with democracy that half the country expects me to wipe my perfectly polished boots on the Cabinet, and the other half expects me to let the Cabinet wipe its muddy boots on me. The Crisis at five o'clock is to decide which of us is to be the doormat.

ORINTHIA: And you will condescend to fight with Proteus for power?

MAGNUS: Oh no: I never fight. But I sometimes win.

ORINTHIA: If you let yourself be beaten by that trickster and poseur, never dare to approach me again.

MAGNUS: Proteus is a clever fellow: even on occasion a fine fellow. It would give me no satisfaction to beat him: I hate beating people. But there would be some innocent fun in outwitting him.

ORINTHIA: Magnus: you are a mollycoddle. If you were a real man you would just delight in beating him to a jelly.

MAGNUS: A real man would never do as a king. I am only an idol, my love; and all I can do is to draw the line at being a cruel idol. [*He looks at his watch*] Now I *must* really be off. Au revoir.

ORINTHIA [*looking at her wrist watch*] But it is only twenty-five minutes past four. You have heaps of time before five.

MAGNUS: Yes; but tea is at half-past four.

ORINTHIA [*catching him by the arm with a snakelike dart*] Never mind your tea. I will give you your tea.

MAGNUS: Impossible, belovéd. Jemima does not like to be kept waiting.

ORINTHIA: Oh, bother Jemima! You shall not leave me to go to Jemima [*she pulls him back so vigorously that he falls into the seat beside her*].

MAGNUS: My dear, I must.

ORINTHIA: No, not today. Listen, Magnus. I have something very particular to say to you.

MAGNUS: You have not. You are only trying to make me late to annoy my wife. [*He tries to rise, but is pulled back*]. Let me go, please.

ORINTHIA [*holding on*] Why are you so afraid of your wife? You are the laughing stock of London, you poor henpecked darling.

MAGNUS: Henpecked! What do you call this? At least my wife does not restrain me by bodily violence.

ORINTHIA: I will not be deserted for your old Dutch.

MAGNUS: Listen, Orinthia. Dont be absurd. You know I must go. Do be good.

ORINTHIA: Only ten minutes more.

MAGNUS: It is half-past already.

He tries to rise; but she holds him back.

MAGNUS [*pausing for breath*] You are doing this out of sheer devilment. You are so abominably strong that I cannot break loose without hurting you. Must I call the guard?

ORINTHIA: Do, do. It will be in all the papers tomorrow.

MAGNUS: Fiend. [*Summoning all his dignity*] Orinthia: I command you.

ORINTHIA [*laughs wildly*]!!!

MAGNUS [*furious*] Very well, then, you she-devil: you shall let go.

He tackles her in earnest. She flings her arms round him and holds on with mischievous enjoyment. There is a tapping at the door; they do not hear it. As he is breaking loose she suddenly shifts her grip to his waist and drags him on to the floor, where they roll over one another. Sempronius enters. He stares at the scandalous scene for a moment; then hastily slips out; shuts the door; clears his throat and blows his nose noisily; and knocks loudly and repeatedly. The two combatants cease hostilities and scramble hastily to their feet.

MAGNUS: Come in.

SEMPRONIUS [*entering*] Her Majesty sent me to remind you that tea is waiting, sir.

MAGNUS: Thank you. [*He goes quickly out*].

ORINTHIA [*panting but greatly pleased with herself*] The King forgets everything when he is here. So do I, I am afraid. I am so sorry.

SEMPRONIUS [*stiffly*] No explanations are needed. I saw what happened. [*He goes out*].

ORINTHIA: The beast! He must have looked through the keyhole. [*She throws her hand up with a gesture of laughing defiance, and dances back to her seat at the writing-table*].

ACT II

Later in the afternoon. The Terrace of the Palace. A low balustrade separates it from the lawn. Terrace chairs in abundance, ranged along the balustrade. Some dining room chairs also, not ranged, but standing about as if they had just been occupied. The terrace is accessible from the lawn by a central flight of steps.

The King and Queen are sitting apart near the corners of the steps, The Queen to the King's right. He is reading the evening paper: she is knitting. She has a little work table on her right, with a small gong on it.

THE QUEEN: Why did you tell them to leave the chairs when they took away the tea?

MAGNUS: I shall receive the Cabinet here.

THE QUEEN: Here! Why?

MAGNUS: Well, I think the open air and the evening light will have a quieting effect on them. They cannot make speeches at me so easily as in a room.

THE QUEEN: Are you sure? When Robert asked Boanerges where he learnt to speak so beautifully, he said 'In Hyde Park.'

MAGNUS: Yes; but with a crowd to stimulate him.

THE QUEEN: Robert says you have tamed Boanerges.

MAGNUS: No: I have not tamed him. I have taught him how to behave. I have to valet all the beginners; but that does not tame them: it teaches them how to use their strength instead of wasting it in making fools of themselves. So much the worse for me when I have to fight them.

THE QUEEN: You get no thanks for it. They think you are only humbugging them.

MAGNUS: Well, so I am, in the elementary lessons. But when it comes to real business humbug is no use: they pick it up themselves too quickly.

Pamphilius enters along the terrace, from The Queen's side.

MAGNUS [*looking at his watch*] Good Heavens! They havnt come, have they? It's not five yet.

PAMPHILIUS: No, sir. It's the American ambassador.

THE QUEEN [*resenting this a little*] Has he an audience?

PAMPHILIUS: No, maam. He is rather excited about something, I think. I cant get anything out of him. He says he must see His Majesty at once.

THE QUEEN: Must!! An American must see the King at once, without an audience! Well!

MAGNUS [*rising*] Send him in, Pam.

Pamphilius goes out.

THE QUEEN: *I* should have told him to write for an audience, and then kept him waiting a week for it.

MAGNUS: What! When we still owe America that old war debt. And with a mad imperialist president like Bossfield! No you wouldnt, my dear: you would be crawlingly civil to him, as I am going to be, confound him!

PAMPHILIUS [*re-appearing*] His Excellency the American Ambassador. Mr. Vanhattan.

He retires as Mr Vanhattan enters in an effusive condition, and, like a man assured of an enthusiastic welcome, hurries to

The Queen, and salutes her with a handshake so prolonged that she stares in astonishment, first at him, and then appealingly at the King, with her hands being vigorously wrung and waved up and down all the time.

MAGNUS: *What on earth is the matter, Mr Vanhattan? You are shaking Her Majesty's rings off.*

VANHATTAN [*desisting*] Her Majesty will excuse me when she learns the nature of my errand here. This, King Magnus, is a great historic scene: one of the greatest, perhaps, that history has ever recorded or will ever again record.

MAGNUS: Have you had tea?

VANHATTAN: Tea! Who can think of tea at such a moment as this?

THE QUEEN [*rather coldly*] It is hard for us to share your enthusiasm in complete ignorance of its cause.

VANHATTAN: That is true, maam. I am just behaving like a crazy man. But you shall hear. You shall judge, and then you shall say whether I exaggerate the importance—the immensity—of an occasion that cannot be exaggerated.

MAGNUS: Goodness gracious! Wont you sit down?

VANHATTAN [*taking a chair and placing it between them*] I thank your Majesty. [*He sits*].

MAGNUS: You have some exciting news for us, apparently. Is it private or official?

VANHATTAN: Official, sir. No mistake about it. What I am going to tell you is authentic from the United States of America to the British Empire.

THE QUEEN: Perhaps I had better go.

VANHATTAN: No, maam: you shall not go. Whatever may be the limits of your privileges as the consort of your sovereign, it is your right as an Englishwoman to learn what I have come here to communicate.

MAGNUS: My dear Vanhattan, what the devil is the matter?

VANHATTAN: King Magnus: between your country and mine there is a debt.

MAGNUS: Does that matter, now that our capitalists have invested so heavily in American concerns that after paying yourselves the interest on the debt you have to send us two thousand million dollars a year to balance the account.

VANHATTAN: King Magnus: for the moment, forget figures. Between your country and mine there is not only a debt but a frontier: the frontier that has on it not a single gun nor a single soldier, and across which the American citizen every day shakes the hand of the Canadian subject of your throne.

MAGNUS: There is also the frontier of the ocean, which is somewhat more expensively defended at our joint expense by the League of Nations.

VANHATTAN [*rising to give his words more impressiveness*] Sir: the debt is cancelled. The frontier no longer exists.

THE QUEEN: How can that be?

MAGNUS: Am I to understand, Mr. Vanhattan, that by some convulsion of Nature the continent of North America has been submerged in the Atlantic?

VANHATTAN: Something even more wonderful than that has happened. One may say that the Atlantic Ocean has been submerged in the British Empire.

MAGNUS: I think you had better tell us as succinctly as possible what has happened. Pray sit down.

VANHATTAN [*resuming his seat*] You are aware, sir, that the United States of America at one time formed a part of your empire.

MAGNUS: There is a tradition to that effect.

VANHATTAN: No mere tradition, sir. An undoubted historical fact. In the eighteenth century—

MAGNUS: That is a long time ago.

VANHATTAN: Centuries count for but little in the lifetimes of great nations, sir. Let me recall the parable of the prodigal son.

MAGNUS: Oh really, Mr. Vanhattan, that was a very very long time ago. I take it that something important has happened since yesterday.

VANHATTAN: It has. It has indeed, King Magnus.

MAGNUS: Then what is it? I have not time to attend to the eighteenth century and the prodigal son at this moment.

THE QUEEN: The King has a Cabinet meeting in ten minutes, Mr. Vanhattan.

VANHATTAN: I should like to see the faces of your Cabinet ministers, King Magnus, when they hear what I have to tell you.

MAGNUS: So should I. But I am not in a position to tell it to them, because I dont know what it is.

VANHATTAN: The prodigal, sir, has returned to his father's house. Not poor, not hungry, not ragged, as of old. Oh no. This time he returns bringing with him the riches of the earth to the ancestral home.

MAGNUS [*starting from his chair*] You dont mean to say—

VANHATTAN [*rising also, blandly triumphant*] I do, sir. The Declaration of Independence is cancelled. The treaties which endorsed it are torn up. We have decided to rejoin the British Empire. We shall of course enjoy Dominion Home Rule under the Presidency of Mr. Bossfield. I shall revisit you here shortly, not as the Ambassador of a foreign power, but as High Commissioner for the greatest of your dominions, and your very loyal and devoted subject, sir.

MAGNUS [*collapsing into his chair*] The devil you will! [*He stares haggardly into futurity, now for the first time utterly at a loss*].

THE QUEEN: What a splendid thing, Mr. Vanhattan!

VANHATTAN: I thought your Majesty would say so. The most splendid thing that has ever happened. [*He resumes his seat*].

THE QUEEN [*looking anxiously at the King*] Dont you think so, Magnus?

MAGNUS [*pulling himself together with a visible effort*] May I ask, Mr Vanhattan, with whom did this—this—this masterstroke of American policy originate? Frankly, I have been accustomed to regard your President as a statesman whose mouth was the most efficient part of his head. He cannot have thought of this himself. Who suggested it to him?

VANHATTAN: I must accept your criticism of Mr Bossfield with all doo reserve, but I may mention that we Americans will probably connect the good news with the recent visit to our shores of the President of the Irish Free State. I cannot pronounce his name in its official Gaelic form; and there is only one typist in our bureau who can spell it; but he is known to his friends as Mick o'Rafferty.

MAGNUS: The rascal! Jemima: we shall have to live in Dublin. This is the end of England.

VANHATTAN: In a sense that may be so. But England will not perish. She will merge—merge, sir—into a bigger and brighter concern. Perhaps I should have mentioned that one of our conditions will be that you shall be Emperor. King may be good enough for this little island; but if we come in we shall require something grander.

MAGNUS: This little island! 'This little gem set in a silver sea!' Has it occurred to you, Mr. Vanhattan, that rather than be reduced to a mere appendage of a big American concern, we might raise the old warcry of Sinn Fein, and fight for our independence to the last drop of our blood?

VANHATTAN: I should be right sorry to contemplate such a reversion to a barbarous past. Fortunately, it's impossible—immpawsibl. The old warcry would not appeal to the cosmopolitan crews of the fleet of the League of Nations in the Atlantic. That fleet would blockade you, sir. And I fear we should be obliged to boycott you. The two thousand million dollars a year would stop.

MAGNUS: But the continental Powers! Do you suppose they would consent for a moment to such a change in the balance of power?

VANHATTAN: Why not? The change would be only nominal.

MAGNUS: Nominal! You call an amalgamation of the British Commonwealth with the United States a nominal change! What will France and Germany call it?

VANHATTAN [*shaking his head indulgently*] France and Germany? These queer old geographical expressions which you use here from old family habit do not trouble us. I suppose you mean by Germany the chain of more or less Soviet Republics between the Ural Mountains and the North Sea. Well, the clever people at Moscow and Berlin and Geneva are trying to federate them; and it is fully understood between us that if we dont object to their move they will not object to ours. France, by which I take it you mean the Government at New Timgad, is too busy in Africa to fuss about what is happening at the ends of your little Channel Tube. So long as Paris is full of Americans, and Americans are full of money, all's well in the west from the French point of view. One of the great attractions of Paris for Americans is the excursion to Old England. The French want us to feel at home here. And so we do. Why shouldnt we? After all, we are at home here.

MAGNUS: In what sense, may I ask?

VANHATTAN: Well, we find here everything we are accustomed to: our industrial products, our books, our plays, our sports, our Christian Science churches, our osteopaths, our movies and talkies. Put it in a small parcel and say our goods and our ideas. A political union with us will be just the official recognition of an already accomplished fact. A union of hearts, you might call it.

THE QUEEN: You forget, Mr. Vanhattan. We have a great national tradition.

VANHATTAN: The United States, maam, have absorbed all the great national traditions, and blended them with their own glorious tradition of Freedom into something that is unique and universal.

THE QUEEN: We have a civilized culture which is peculiar to ourselves. It may not be better than yours; but it is different.

VANHATTAN: Well, is it? We found that culture enshrined in British material works of art: in the stately country homes of your nobility, in the cathedrals our common forefathers built as the country houses of God. What did you do with them? You sold them to us. I was brought up in the shade of Ely cathedral, the removal of which from the county of Cambridge to New Jersey was my dear old father's first big professional job. The building which stands on its former site is a very fine one: in my opinion the best example of reinforced concrete of its period; but it was designed by an American architect, and built by the Synthetic Building Materials Trust, an international affair. Believe me, the English people, the real English people who take things as they come instead of reading books about them, will be more at home with us than they are with the old English notions which our tourists try to keep alive. When you find some country gentleman keeping up the old English customs at Christmas and so forth, who is he? An American who has bought the place. Your people get up the show for him because he pays for it, not because it is natural to them.

THE QUEEN [*with a sigh*] Our own best families go so much to Ireland nowadays. People should not be allowed to go from England to Ireland. They never come back.

VANHATTAN: Well, can you blame them, maam? Look at the climate!

THE QUEEN: No: it is not the climate. It is the Horse Show.

The King rises very thoughtfully; and Vanhattan follows his example.

MAGNUS: I must think over this. I have known for years past that it was on the cards. When I was young, and under the influence of our family tradition, which of course never recognized the rebellion of the American colonies as valid, I actually dreamt of a reunited English speaking empire at the head of civilization.

VANHATTAN: Fine! Great! And now come true.

MAGNUS: Not yet. Now that I am older and wiser I find the reality less attractive than the dream.

VANHATTAN: And is that all I am to report to the President, sir? He will be disappointed. I am a little taken aback, myself.

MAGNUS: For the present, that is all. This may be a great idea—

VANHATTAN: Surely, surely.

MAGNUS: It may also be a trap in which England will perish.

VANHATTAN [*encouragingly*] Oh, I shouldnt look at it that way. Besides, nothing—not even dear old England—can last for ever. Progress, you know, sir, progress, progress!

MAGNUS: Just so, just so. We may survive only as another star on your flag. Still, we cling to the little scrap of individuality you have left us. If we must merge, as you call it—or did you say submerge? — some of us will swim to the last. [*To The Queen*] My dear.

The Queen strikes her gong.

Pamphilius returns.

MAGNUS: You shall hear from me after the Cabinet meets. Not tonight: you must not sit up waiting for a message. Early tomorrow, I hope. Thank you for bringing me the news before the papers got it: that seldom happens now. Pamphilius: you will reconduct his Excellency. Good evening. [*He shakes hands*].

VANHATTAN: I thank your Majesty. [*To the Queen*] Good evening, maam. I look forward to presenting myself in court dress soon.

THE QUEEN: You will look very nice in it, Mr. Vanhattan. Good evening.

The Ambassador goes out with Pamphilius.

MAGNUS [*striding grimly to and fro*] The scoundrels! That blackguard o'Rafferty! That booby bullroarer Bossfield! Breakages, Limited, have taken it into their heads to mend the British Commonwealth.

THE QUEEN [*quietly*] I think it is a very good thing. You will make a very good emperor. We shall civilize these Americans.

MAGNUS: How can we when we have not yet civilized ourselves? They have come to regard us as a mere tribe of redskins. England will be just a reservation.

THE QUEEN: Nonsense, dear! They know that we are their natural superiors. You can see it by the way their women behave at court. They really love and reverence royalty; while our English peeresses are hardly civil—when they condescend to come at all.

MAGNUS: Well, my dear, I do many things to please you that I should never do to please myself; and I suppose I shall end as American Emperor just to keep you amused.

THE QUEEN: I never desire anything that is not good for you, Magnus. You do not always know what is good for you.

MAGNUS: Well, well, well, well! Have it your own way, dearest. Where are these infernal ministers? Theyre late.

THE QUEEN [*looking out into the garden*] Coming across the lawn with Sempronius.

The Cabinet arrives. The men take off their hats as they come up the steps. Boanerges has taken advantage of the interval to procure a brilliant uniform and change into it. Proteus, with Sempronius, heads the procession, followed immediately by the two lady ministers. The Queen rises as Proteus turns to her. Sempronius moves the little table quickly back to the balustrade out of the way, and puts The Queen's chair in the centre for the King.

THE QUEEN [*shaking hands*] How do you do, Mr. Proteus?

PROTEUS: May I present the President of the Board of Trade, Mr. Boanerges?

THE QUEEN: I remember seeing you, Mr. Boanerges, at the opening of the Transport Workers' Summer Palace. You wore a most becoming costume then. I hope you have not given it up.

BOANERGES: But the Princess told me I looked ridiculous in it!

THE QUEEN: That was very naughty of the Princess. You looked particularly well in it. However, you look well in anything. And now I leave you all to your labors.

She goes out along the terrace. Sempronius follows with her knitting.

MAGNUS [*sitting down*] Be seated, ladies and gentlemen.

They take chairs of one sort or another where they can find them, first leaving their hats on the balustrade. When they are seated, their order from the King's right to his left is Nicobar, Crassus, Boanerges, Amanda, the King, Proteus, Lysistrata, Pliny, and Balbus.

A pause, Proteus waiting for the King to begin. He, deep in thought, says nothing. The silence becomes oppressive.

PLINY [*chattily*] Nice weather we're having, these evenings.

AMANDA [*splutters*]!!!

MAGNUS: There is rather a threatening cloud on the western horizon, Mr Pliny: [*To Proteus*] Have you heard the news from America?

PROTEUS: I have, sir.

MAGNUS: Am I to be favored with the advice of my ministers on that subject?

PROTEUS: By your Majesty's leave, we will take the question of the ultimatum first.

MAGNUS: Do you think the ultimatum will matter much when the capital of the British Commonwealth is shifted to Washington?

NICOBAR: We'll see it shifted to Melbourne or Montreal or Johannesburg first.

MAGNUS: It would not stay there. It will stay at a real centre of gravity only.

PROTEUS: We are agreed about that. If it shifts at all it will shift either west to Washington or east to Moscow.

BOANERGES: Moscow thinks a lot of itself. But what has Moscow to teach us that we cannot teach ourselves? Moscow is built on English history, written in London by Karl Marx.

PROTEUS: Yes; and the English king has sidetracked you again. [*To Magnus*] What about the ultimatum, sir? You promised us your decision at five o'clock. It is now a quarter past.

MAGNUS: Are you inexorably determined to force this issue to its logical end? You know how unEnglish it is to do that?

PROTEUS: My people came from Scotland.

LYSISTRATA: I wish they had stayed there. I am English: every bone in my body.

BOANERGES [*vociferously*] Same here!

PROTEUS: God help England if she had no Scots to think for her!

MAGNUS: What does the Cabinet say to that?

AMANDA: All their people came from Scotland or Ireland or Wales or Jerusalem or somewhere, sir. It is no use appealing to English sentiment here.

CRASSUS: Politics are not suited to the English, if you ask me.

MAGNUS: Then I, the only Englishman left in politics, apparently, am to be reduced to complete nullity?

PROTEUS [*bluntly*] Yes. You cannot frighten us out of our position by painting it red. I could paint your position black if I liked. In plain terms we require from you an unconditional surrender. If you refuse it then I go to the country on the question whether England is to be an absolute monarchy or a constitutional one. We are all agreed on that: there will be no resignations. I have letters from the absent members of the Government: those present will speak for themselves.

ALL THE OTHER MEN. Agreed, agreed.

PROTEUS: Now, what is your answer?

MAGNUS: The day for absolute monarchies is past. You think you can do without me; and I know that I cannot do without you. I decide, of course, in favor of a constitutional monarchy.

THE MEN [*greatly relieved and delighted*] Hear! hear!

MAGNUS: Wait a moment.

Sudden silence and mistrust.

PROTEUS: So! There is a catch in it, is there?

MAGNUS: Not exactly a catch. But you have driven me to face the fact that I am unfitted to be a constitutional monarch. I am by nature incapable of the necessary self-effacement.

AMANDA: Well, thats true, at all events. You and I are a pair, sir.

MAGNUS: Thank you. Therefore, whilst accepting your constitutional principle without the slightest reserve, I cannot sign your ultimatum, because by doing so I should be making personal promises which I know I should break—which in fact I must break because I have forces within me which your constitutional limits cannot hold in check.

BALBUS: How can you accept our principle if you dont sign the ultimatum?

MAGNUS: Oh, there is no difficulty about that. When an honest man finds himself incapable of discharging the duties of a public post, he resigns.

PROTEUS [*alarmed*] Resigns! What are you driving at?

CRASSUS: A king cannot resign.

NICOBAR: You might as well talk of beheading yourself. You cant behead yourself.

BOANERGES: Other people can, though.

MAGNUS: Do not let us quarrel about words, gentlemen. I cannot resign. But I can abdicate.

ALL THE REST [*starting to their feet*] Abdicate! [*They stare at him in consternation*].

AMANDA [*whistling a descending minor scale very expressively*] !!!!!!!! [*She sits down*].

MAGNUS: Of course, abdicate. Lysistrata: you have been a teacher of history. You can assure your colleagues that there is nothing unprecedented in an abdication. The Emperor Charles the Fifth, for instance—

LYSISTRATA: Oh, Charles the Fifth be—be bothered! he's not good enough. Sir: I have stood by you as far as I dared. Dont throw me over. You must not abdicate. [*She sits down, distressed*].

PROTEUS: You cannot abdicate except by my advice.

MAGNUS: I am acting upon your advice.

PROTEUS: Nonsense! [*He sits down*].

BALBUS: Ridiculous! [*He sits down*].

PLINY: Youre not serious, you know. [*He sits down*].

NICOBAR: You cant upset the apple cart like this. [*He sits down*].

CRASSUS: I must say this is not playing the game. [*He sits down*].

BOANERGES [*powerfully*] Well, why not? Why not? Though as an old Republican I have no respect for His Majesty as a King, I have a great respect for him as a Strong Man. But he is not the only pebble on the beach. Why not have done with this superstition of monarchy, and bring the British

Commonwealth into line with all the other great Powers today as a republic? [*He sits down*].

MAGNUS: My abdication does not involve that, Mr Boanerges. I am abdicating to save the monarchy, not to destroy it. I shall be succeeded by my son Robert, Prince of Wales. He will make an admirable constitutional monarch.

PLINY: Oh, come! Dont be hard on the lad, sir. He has plenty of brains.

MAGNUS: Oh yes, yes, yes: I did not mean that he is a nonentity. quite the contrary: he is much cleverer than I am. But I have never been able to induce him to take any interest in parliamentary politics. He prefers intellectual pursuits.

NICOBAR: Dont you believe it. He is up to his neck in business.

MAGNUS: Just so. He asks me why I waste my time with you here pretending to govern the country when it is really governed by Breakages, Limited. And really I hardly know how to answer him.

CRASSUS: Things are like that nowadays. My son says just the same.

LYSISTRATA: Personally I get on very well with the Prince; but somehow I do not feel that he is interested in what I am doing.

BALBUS: He isnt. He wont interfere with you as long as you dont interfere with him. Just the right king for us. Not pig-headed. Not meddlesome. Thinks that nothing we do matters a rap. What do you say, Joe?

PROTEUS: After all, why not? if your Majesty is in earnest.

MAGNUS: I assure you I am very much in earnest.

PROTEUS: Well, I confess I did not foresee this turn of events. But I ought to have foreseen it. What your Majesty proposes is the straightforward, logical, intellectually honest solution of our difficulty. Consequently it is the last solution I could have expected in politics. But I reckoned without your Majesty's character. The more I think of it the more clearly I see that you are right—that you are taking the only course open to you.

CRASSUS: I never said I was against it, Joe.

BALBUS: Neither did I.

NICOBAR: I think theres a great deal to be said for it. I have no objection.

PLINY: One king is no worse than another, is he?

BOANERGES: Is he any better? The way you fellows scuttle backward and forward from one mind to another whenever Joe holds up his finger is disgusting. This is a Cabinet of sheep.

PROTEUS: Well, give the flock a better lead if you can. Have you anything else to propose?

BOANERGES: I dont know that I have on the spur of the moment. We should have had notice of this. But I suppose the King must do as he thinks right.

PROTEUS: Then the goat goes with the sheep; so thats all right.

BOANERGES: Who are you calling a goat?

NICOBAR: If you come to that, who are you calling sheep?

AMANDA: Steady there, children! steady! steady! [*To the King*] You have brought us all round, sir, as usual.

PROTEUS: There is nothing more to be said.

AMANDA: That means another half hour at least.

BOANERGES: Woman: this is not the moment for your tomfooleries.

PROTEUS [*impressively*] Bill is right, Amanda. [*He rises and becomes the conventional House of Commons orator*].

Ministers compose themselves to listen with grave attention, as if in church; but Lysistrata is contemptuous and Amanda amused.

PROTEUS [*continuing*] It is a solemn moment. It is a moment in which an old tie is being broken. I am not ashamed to confess that it is a tie from which I have learned something.

MALE MINISTERS [*murmur*] Hear hear! Hear hear!

PROTEUS: For my own part—and I think I may speak for others here as well—it has been no mere political tie, but a tie of sincere friendship.

Renewed murmurs of sympathy. Increasing emotion.

PROTEUS: We have had our disagreements—as which of us has not?—but they have been family quarrels.

CRASSUS: Thats all. Nothing more.

PROTEUS: May I say lovers' quarrels?

PLINY [*wiping his eyes*] You may, Joe. You may.

PROTEUS: My friends, we came here to a meeting. We find, alas! that the meeting is to be a leavetaking. [*Crassus sniffs tearfully*]. It is a sad leavetaking on our part, but a cordial one. [Hear Hear *from Pliny*]. We are cast down, but not discouraged. Looking back to the past with regret, we can still look forward to the future with hope. That future has its dangers and its difficulties. It will bring us new problems; and it will bring us face to face with a new king. But the new problems and the new king will not make us forget our old counsellor, monarch, and—he will allow me to say—comrade. [Hear Hears *ad libitum*]. I know my words will find an echo in all your hearts when I conclude by saying that whatsoever king shall reign—

AMANDA: Youll be the Vicar of Bray, Joe.

Uproar. Proteus flings himself into his chair indignantly.

BALBUS: Shame!

NICOBAR: Shut up, you b—

PLINY: A joke's a joke; but really—

CRASSUS: Too bad, Amanda! Behave yourself.

LYSISTRATA: She has a perfect right to speak. You are a parcel of sentimental fools.

BOANERGES [*rising*] Silence. Order.

AMANDA: Sorry.

BOANERGES: So you ought to be. Where's your manners? Where's your education? King Magnus: we part; but we part as strong men part: as friends. The Prime Minister has correctly represented the sentiments of all the men present. I call on them to express those sentiments in the good old English fashion. [*Singing in stentorian tones*] Fo-o-o-o-r-r-r-

MALE MINISTERS EXCEPT PROTEUS [*rising and singing*]

—he's a jolly good fel-low
For he's a jolly good fel-low
For he's—

MAGNUS [*peremptorily*] Stop. Stop.

Sudden silence and misgiving. They sit down furtively.

MAGNUS: I thank you with all my heart; but there is a misapprehension. We are not taking leave of one another. I have no intention of withdrawing from an active part in politics.

PROTEUS: What!!

MAGNUS: You are looking on me, with an emotion which has deeply touched me, as a man with a political past. But I look on myself rather as a man with a political future. I have not yet told you my plans.

NICOBAR: What plans?

BALBUS: A retired king cant have plans and a future.

MAGNUS: Why not? I am looking forward to a most exciting and enjoyable time. As I shall of course dissolve parliament, the fun will begin with a general election.

BOANERGES [*dismayed*] But Ive only just been elected. Do you mean that I shall have to stand two elections in one month? Have you thought of the expenses?

MAGNUS: Surely your expenses will be paid by the State.

BOANERGES: Paid by the State! Is that all you know about electioneering in England?

PROTEUS: You will get your whack out of the party funds, Bill; and if you cant find the extras you must put up with straight votes. Go on, sir: we want to hear about those plans of yours.

MAGNUS: My last act of royal authority will be to divest myself of all titles and dignities; so that I may step down at once into the position of a commoner.

BOANERGES: Step up, you mean. The common man is the superior, not the inferior, of the titled man.

MAGNUS: That is why I am going to make myself a common man, Mr Boanerges.

PLINY: Well, it does you honor.

CRASSUS: Not all of us would be capable of a sacrifice like that.

BOANERGES: A fine gesture, sir. A fine gesture. I admit it.

PROTEUS [*suspicious*] And since when, pray, has your Majesty taken to making gestures? Whats the game this time?

BOANERGES: Shame!

PROTEUS: Shut up, you gaby. [*To the King*] I say, whats the game?

MAGNUS: There is no imposing on you, Prime Minister. The game is, of course, that when I come back into politics

I shall be in a better position as a commoner than as a peer. I shall seek a parliamentary seat.

PROTEUS: You in the House of Commons!

MAGNUS [*blandly*] It is my intention to offer myself to the Royal Borough of Windsor as a candidate at the forthcoming General Election.

All the rest except Boanerges and the ladies rise in consternation.

PROTEUS: This is treachery.

BALBUS: A dirty trick.

NICOBAR: The meanest on record.

PLINY: He'll be at the top of the poll.

CRASSUS: There wont be any poll: it will be a walkover.

BALBUS: This shews what all your fine manners and friendly ways are worth.

NICOBAR: Hypocrite!

CRASSUS: Humbug!

LYSISTRATA: I wish your Majesty every success.

AMANDA: Hear hear! Fair play, boys. Why shouldnt he go into parliament with us?

BOANERGES: Well said! well said! Why not?

THE OTHER MALE MINISTERS. Ya-a-a-ah! [*They sit down in utter disgust*].

PROTEUS [*very sullen*] And when you are in Parliament, what then?

MAGNUS: There are several possibilities. I shall naturally endeavor to form a party. My son King Robert will have to call on some Party leader who can depend on the support of the House of Commons to form a Government: He may call on you. He may even call on me.

AMANDA [*breaks the glum silence by whistling a bar or two of the National Anthem*]!!

MAGNUS: Whatever happens, it will be a great relief to us to be able to speak out quite frankly about one another in public. You have never been able to tell the British people what you really think of me: no real criticism of the King is possible. I have never been able to speak my mind as to your various capacities and characters. All that reserve, that tedious affectation, that unwholesome concealment will end. I hope you look forward to our new footing as pleasurably as I do.

LYSISTRATA: I am delighted, sir. You will fight Breakages for me.

AMANDA: It will be awful fun.

BOANERGES: Now, Mr Prime Minister, we are waiting for you. What have you to say about it?

PROTEUS [*rising and speaking slowly, with his brows deeply knitted*] Has Your Majesty got that ultimatum on you?

MAGNUS [*produces it from his breast pocket and presents it to him*]!

PROTEUS [*with measured emphasis, after tearing the paper up into four pieces at two deliberate strokes, and throwing the pieces away*] There is not going to be any abdication. There is not going to be any general election. There is not going to be any ultimatum. We go on as before. The crisis is a washout. [*To the King, with deadly concentration*] I will never forgive you for this. You stole your ace of trumps from the hand I played this morning. [*He takes his hat from the balustrade and goes away through the park*].

BOANERGES [*rising*] That was a very deplorable exhibition of temper on the part of the Prime Minister, sir. It was not the gesture of a Strong Man. I will remonstrate with him. You may depend on me. [*He takes his hat and follows Proteus in a serious and dignified manner*].

NICOBAR [*rising*] Well, I shall not say what I think. [*He is taking his hat when the King addresses him*].

MAGNUS: So I have not upset the apple cart after all, Mr Nicobar.

NICOBAR: You can upset it as soon as you like for all I care. I am going out of politics. Politics is a mug's game. [*He goes*].

CRASSUS [*rising reluctantly and taking his hat*] If Nick goes, I shall have to go too.

MAGNUS: Can you really tear yourself away from politics?

CRASSUS: Only too glad to be well out of them, if Breakages will let me. They shoved me into it; and I daresay theyll find another job for me. [*He goes*].

PLINY [*cheerful to the last as he, too, goes for his hat*] Well, I am glad nothing's happened. You know, sir, nothing ever really does happen in the Cabinet. Never mind their bit of temper. Theyll feed out of your hand tomorrow. [*He goes*].

BALBUS [*after taking his hat*] Now that theyre all gone I dont mind saying that if anything should ever happen to the throne, and your Majesty should become a President with a Cabinet to pick, you might easily find a worse Home Secretary than me, with all my faults.

MAGNUS: I shall bear it in mind. By the way, if you should happen to overtake the Prime Minister, will you be so good as to remind him that we quite forgot to settle that little affair of the proposal of America to annex the British Commonwealth.

BALBUS: By the Lord, so we did! Well, thats a good one! Ha ha! Ha ha ha ha ha! [*He goes out laughing heartily*].

MAGNUS: They dont take it in, Lizzie: not one bit. It is as if another planet were crashing into us. The kingdom and the power and the glory will pass from us and leave us naked, face to face with our real selves at last.

LYSISTRATA: So much the better, if by our real selves you mean the old English stock that was unlike any other. Nowadays men all over the world are as much alike as hotel dinners. It's no use pretending that the America of George Washington is going to swallow up the England of Queen Anne. The America of George Washington is as dead as Queen Anne. What they call an American is only a wop pretending to be a Pilgrim Father. He is no more Uncle Jonathan than you are John Bull.

MAGNUS: Yes: we live in a world of wops, all melting into one another; and when all the frontiers are down London may be outvoted by Tennessee, and all the other places where we still madly teach our children the mentality of an eighteenth century village school.

LYSISTRATA: Never fear, sir. It is not the most ignorant national crowd that will come out on top, but the best power station; for you cant do without power stations, and you cant run them on patriotic songs and hatred of the foreigner, and guff and bugaboo, though you can run nationalism on nothing else. But I am heartbroken at your not coming into the House with us to keep old England in front and lead a new Party against Breakages [*tears come into her eyes*].

MAGNUS [*patting her consolingly on the back*] That would have been splendid, wouldnt it? But I am too old fashioned. This is a farce that younger men must finish.

AMANDA [*taking her arm*] Come home with me, dear. I will sing to you until you cant help laughing. Come.

Lysistrata pockets her handkerchief; shakes the King's hands impulsively; and goes with Amanda: The King plunges into deep thought. Presently The Queen comes back.

THE QUEEN: Now Magnus: it's time to dress for dinner.

MAGNUS [*much disturbed*] Oh, not now. I have something very big to think about. I dont want any dinner.

THE QUEEN [*peremptorily*] No dinner! Did anyone ever hear of such a thing! You know you will not sleep if you think after seven o'clock.

MAGNUS [*worried*] But really, Jemima—

THE QUEEN [*going to him and taking his arm*] Now, now, now! dont be naughty. I musnt be late for dinner. Come on, like a good little boy.

The King, with a grimace of hopeless tenderness, allows himself to be led away.

George Bernard Shaw, (26th July, 1856, Dublin, Ireland—2nd November, 1950, Hertfordshire, England), was an Irish playwright, author, literary critic, political activist, socialist propagandist, and the winner of the Nobel Prize for Literature in 1925. He was the third and youngest child (and only son) of George Carr Shaw and Lucinda Elizabeth Gurly Shaw. Technically, he belonged to the Protestant ascendancy, the landed Irish gentry, but his impractical father was first a sinecure civil servant and then an unsuccessful grain merchant. Therefore, he grew up in an atmosphere of genteel poverty, which to him was more humiliating than being merely poor. At first, he was tutored by his clerical uncle, then he was sent to various schools in Dublin but developed a great dislike for the formalized education systems.

Shaw developed a wide knowledge of music, art, and literature as a result of his mother's influence and his visits to the National Gallery of Ireland. After working in an estate agent's office for a while, in 1876, he left for London to join his mother. In London, he established himself as a leading music and theatre critic in the eighties and nineties and became a prominent member of the Fabian Society, for which he composed many pamphlets. With fellow Fabians such as Sidney and Beatrice Webb, he played an important role in the foundation of the London School of Economics (LSE) after receiving private bequests.

Shaw began his literary career as a novelist and as a fervent advocate of the new theatre of Ibsen (*The Quintessence of Ibsenism,* 1891) he decided to write plays in order to illustrate his criticism of the English stage. By the 1890s, his plays were being performed in London and the income from his plays enabled him to devote his life to writing. Like his contemporary, Oscar Wilde, his plays were popular for their biting wit and humour. His plays were in contrast to many Victorian plays which tended to be sentimental, escapist, and lacking in satire. His earliest dramas were called appropriately Plays Pleasant and Unpleasant (1898). Among these, *Widower's Houses and Mrs. Warren's Profession* savagely attack social hypocrisy, while in plays such as *Arms and the Man and The Man of Destiny* the criticism is less fierce. His radical rationalism, his utter disregard of conventions, his keen dialectic interest and verbal wit often turn the stage into a forum of ideas.